The Story of John

Chelsea Curtis Fraser

Alpha Editions

This edition published in 2024

ISBN : 9789362926753

Design and Setting By
Alpha Editions
www.alphaedis.com
Email - info@alphaedis.com

Contents

PREFACE

For a corking tale of the sea it would be hard to find in all fiction a story to equal that of John Paul Jones, a figure of sober history. Yet history was not so "sober" after all, in those days when piracy was an actual fact, and even nations at times winked at privateering on the high seas. Jones was born with a love of the salt spray in his nostrils. He came to this country as a mere lad, but already a skilled sailor. When the Revolution broke out, he obtained command of a ship, and was the first to fly the Stars-and-Stripes in foreign waters. Then came his deeds of daring against the British Navy, and his repeated victories over tremendous odds. The fight between the *Bon Homme Richard* and the *Serapis* is a classic. "Surrender?" he cried with most of his rigging shot away, and his vessel sinking, "Why, I have just begun to fight!"

Belated honors were done to his memory, a few years ago, when his body was brought home from a neglected grave in France, and reinterred at Annapolis with all the honors in the gift of the nation. When the readers young and old lay aside this thrilling story, they also will understand why America honors his memory. He may be regarded as the founder of the United States Navy. His flag, whether flying at the masthead of some saucy little sloop-of-war or on a more formidable ship of the line, never knew what it was to be hauled down in defeat. His name has become a tradition among all sea fighters.

I

THE STORM

In the summer of 1759, James Younger, a prosperous shipowning merchant of Whitehaven, England, found himself short of sailors to man a new vessel he had just secured. Said he to himself, "I know just where I shall be likely to pick up such fellows as I need. To-morrow I shall go to Arbigland."

Arbigland was a small fishing-village directly across the Solway Firth, a sort of big bay which cuts a wedge into the borderline of Scotland and England and reaches out into the blueness of the Irish Sea. From this port fishing-boats in great numbers were wont to go forth in the early morning of the day and return at sunset with their catch. Practically every home was the hearth of a fisherman and his family—sturdy, weather-beaten men who knew the whims of a boat and the tricks of the sea better than they knew how to read and write; sturdy, hard-working mothers who knew more about baking bread and rearing good children than they did about social functions and social etiquette; sturdy lads and lassies who lived in the open and knew more about entertaining themselves with the rugged and wholesome interests of nature than they did about ball-rooms, wine suppers, and "movies." From Arbigland Mr. Younger had more than once before obtained excellent sailors, as had indeed many another ship-merchant and short-handed captain.

Mr. Younger's hopes of securing good seamen in Arbigland were soon fulfilled. He found no trouble in signing up nearly enough that very evening, among them several officers. The following morning he completed his list, but did not attempt an immediate return to Whitehaven on account of bad weather. That day the winds increased and the sea became constantly more and more violent. By mid-afternoon the waves were running so high that the fishermen who had gone out came scurrying in, glad to find a safe anchorage in the harbor.

Seeing a knot of idlers gathered on the waterfront, he joined them to find out what they were looking at. Not until one of them had painstakingly pointed out to him a small object, now in view on the crest of a mountainous wave, now vanished from sight in the trough of another, did he suspect that it could be a boat that had failed to get in.

"It's Johnnie Paul and his little dory, I be sure," observed one of the fishermen, who held a glass to his eyes. "It looks fair bad f'r the lad this time, an' na mistake. It's gude his ain faither don't ken the boy's peril."

"On'y twelve—a mere baby—an' him a-fightin' this nor'easter!" put in another fisherman, with a sorrowful shake of his grizzled head. "T'bad Johnnie's recklessness should 'a' got him in this fix. I'm afraid the lad's love for the sea will spell his doom this blow. He's a muckle bright lad, too."

"An' a born seaman. If a lad are ever born to the sea Johnnie Paul are that chap," said another Scotsman in tarpaulin. "Mind ye, boys, we seen him make port afore in stoorms a'most this bad. Mayhap he'll do it noo. He's got the luck o' the devil in his small frame, that he has!"

Whether it was "the luck of the devil" or just plain unvarnished skill which brought Johnnie Paul safely into port again that day will probably never be known. But the chances are, if luck entered into the matter at all, that good seamanship and intrepid daring performed the largest share of the performance, for, as the minutes went on and the small boat came bobbing nearer and nearer, it was evident to every one of those assembled seafaring men that the youngster was handling his steed with unusual cleverness. Virtually flying in the very face of disaster and death, the lad clung coolly to the tiller, his eyes snapping with excitement, his dark-brown hair tossing, while the vicious nor'easter almost tore his reefed sail from its fastenings, drenched him to the skin with its wild spray, and drove his cockleshell of a craft swiftly forward.

Held spellbound by the struggle between boy and wave, thrilled at the magnificence of the lad's courage and the adroitness of his movements as his tiller-hand avoided yawning danger after yawning danger, Mr. Younger found himself praying for the safety of the daring young boatman, as he might have prayed for the deliverance of one of his own children from such a threatened fate. And it was with a vast sense of relief and thankfulness that, a little later, he saw Johnnie Paul guide his frail vessel into the protected waters of the harbor and up to the wharf, where she was securely made fast.

Indeed, Mr. Younger was one of the very first to shake the hand of the dripping boy and congratulate him on his splendid performance. "If I mistake not, one of these days you will be a great sailor, my lad," said he, little knowing that he was predicting a truth.

Johnnie Paul blushed painfully. But quickly the snap and sparkle returned to his hazel eyes. "Sir, it is what I should like to be—a great sailor," he said.

Other words followed. "I shall see your father. Perhaps we can induce him to let you join one of my vessels," observed the ship-owner from

Whitehaven. "You are very young, but old enough to become an apprentice or ship's-boy."

Young John Paul ran home as fast as his legs could carry him, his heart beating with joy. Oh, such luck! It seemed to him he had always wanted to be a sailor—a real sailor, one who could tread a big vessel's deck, climb her rigging, and go far out to sea past that misty blue line that separated home waters from the mystery and adventure of the domain lying leagues beyond.

Since he was a mere baby he recalled that he had always had a passion to sail something, even so simple a thing as a leaf, the half of a walnut shell, a bit of wood supporting a paper sail. And, in the beginning, the duck-pond, a horse-trough, or a puddle of rainwater, had been his sea. But he outgrew these limitations as he outgrew his kilts: more room must be provided for his bounding spirits and expanding ambition. Then had come first thoughts of the seashore; father's and mother's warnings that the strong tides of the Solway were too dangerous to play with, had only increased his desire to tussle with them. So he had run away, been sternly chastised, had run away again—until at length, despairing of restraining his son from the natural craving of his heart, John Paul senior threw away his switch and left the youngster to the care of Providence whenever his footsteps prompted him waterward.

As time went on, young John had grown into a sturdy lad whose chief delight was to sail off in the fishermen's boats for a day's catch. What he dreamed, what he planned, as he watched the far horizon, no one knows, for he was not the kind of a boy to tell others of his inner thoughts at that age. But that he did have frequent golden dreams we may rest assured, since, between the times he was making himself useful in casting and hauling in the nets, his older comrades often caught him in abstracted study of distant spaces.

In those days Scottish schools were not what they are now. There were very few of them then, and the instruction had not begun to reach the thoroughness it has since attained. Less than a dozen children attended the little school in Arbigland to which Johnnie Paul had been consigned at the age of eight. It was so difficult to get a teacher that sometimes for weeks at a time there was no one to hold forth in that office. These occasions were very satisfying to our Johnnie Paul, for the truth is, he much preferred paddling around the water to fingering over the pages of his books. But he was not lazy, and during the short time he did spend under the roof of a schoolhouse, he must have applied himself, for the records show that at twelve years of age he could figure and read and write very well indeed for that period.

The lad's mother had been Jean Macduff, the daughter of an Argyll Highlander who had moved into the Lowlands, there to abandon his trade of armorer and become a farmer near New Abbey. Jean Macduff later left her home and came to Arbigland to accept a position as lady's-maid to a Mrs. Craik whose husband was a prosperous land-owner possessing an extensive estate and splendid buildings on top of the promontory hanging above the shores of the Solway.

When quite a young man, John's father, a Lowlander, had also found employment on the Craik estate as gardener, and later by reason of his faithful work and popularity in the community, he had been made game-warden. The young gardener and the young lady's-maid soon fell in love with each other, were married, and in due course of time were blessed with five children, of whom Johnnie was the youngest. He was born in the year 1747. William, the brother, had gone to live with a cousin, William Jones, a childless planter in Virginia, before John was born. Willie had never been back since that day. He had been adopted by the distant cousin, and might never return, John's parents said, but it was hoped and expressed in letters that he would some of these days make the long voyage back to old Scotland for a brief visit. How Johnnie did yearn to see this big brother whose letters he loved to read but whom he had never seen! Of late he had even dared to think of making a voyage himself to American shores, there to seek out the long-absent one.

The Paul cottage, overgrown with creepers, and sheltered from the fierce northeast winds by thick trees and shrubbery, stood so close to the seashore that it was never free from the sound of lapping waters and the boom of breakers. It was the boy's delight, before he went to sleep of a night, and before he arose of a morning, to lie for some time and listen to the music of the waves, his vivid fancy investing these voices with the power of telling him strange tales of strange peoples and strange places, far, far away.

When young John was not on the water, in school, or at home, he could usually be found somewhere about Mr. Craik's estate. He was kindly treated, and the playmate of the sons of the good laird's family. With the democracy of boyhood he and the Craik lads enjoyed climbing everything in the neighborhood, from the highest trees to the most rugged cliffs, where lurked unexplored treasures in the shape of sea-birds' eggs. They penetrated caves and caverns under the cliffs with that sublime disregard of tides which is boyhood's happy prerogative. They lingered at the hearths of Old Elspeth and Meg Merrilies, in the valley below, drinking in tales of elf and goblin—too frightened to go home in the dusk, until the servants of the big house finally hunted up and retrieved them.

And now all this commonplace existence was to be traded off for the more alluring one of a sailor's life—if only the stranger from Whitehaven did not forget to keep his word and ask Johnnie Paul's father and mother to permit him to go off to sea—and if that father and mother could be prevailed upon to give their consent!

Young John had never covered the distance from the waterfront to his humble home as quickly as he had that stormy afternoon following his meeting with Mr. James Younger. There he shouted the news to his shocked mother, and then, still in his wet garments, ran over to the Craik estate and told his father and Mr. Craik himself.

Had not the latter interceded in his behalf at the last moment it is doubtful if John Paul senior and his good wife would ever have allowed Johnnie to go, when Mr. Younger called that evening and presented the case to them. As it was, they finally agreed that their youngest son should become an apprentice to the Whitehaven ship-owner.

Then John Paul was indeed a happy boy. He did not sleep a wink that night. All through the long hours he lay listening to the lashing waves. They had never sounded so sweet before.

II

THE LAND ACROSS THE SEA

"Gude-by, mither! Gude-by, faither! Gude-by, dear sisters!"

The big ship which had brought Mr. James Younger to Arbigland in quest of sailors tugged restlessly at her anchor-chains in the river. Her sails were being unfurled to the fresh breeze by her crew. The storm of the day before had subsided during the night, and all was ready for the departure.

Already a yawl-load of newly-engaged seamen had reached the vessel's deck. And now, with a little bundle under his arm and the kisses of his kinsfolk still warm on his cheek, young Johnnie Paul courageously tried to keep back the lump that seemed bound to rise in his throat, and stepped into the last ship's-boat with Mr. Younger himself. As the oarsmen bent to their task and the boat left the dock farther and farther behind, John waved his hand to the group on the shore. Beside his own household Mr. Craik's family were gathered there to see him off, also every man, woman, and child in the village. He knew them all. Every one was sorry to see him go, and all wished the lad they loved God-speed.

John had not fancied his eyes would blur this way when the final parting should come. He had never been away from home before in all his twelve years of life. It is no wonder that for a short time he had an impulse to ask Mr. Younger to turn about and leave him behind.

But fortunately for the country in which American children live, this Scotch lad steeled himself into seeing his bargain through, be it for better or for worse. So he maintained a steadfast silence, gazed straight ahead at the scurrying sailors aboard the big ship, which was now quite close, and, quickly absorbed in their movements, soon recovered his enthusiasm for the project upon which he had entered. Landlubber though they might call him, he determined to show these tars that he was no stranger to the ways, whims and tricks of water even if he were unused to handling a big vessel.

Two hours later the high cliffs marking the site of Arbigland were all that young John could see of the little fishing-village. They were well out in the Solway, plowing their way toward Whitehaven, on the adjoining English coast. The sea was still quite rough—rough enough to have made any lad unused to the rolling motion of a boat prodigiously seasick. Not so Johnnie Paul. To the disappointment of a number of the old salts who expected to have sport with him in this way, John went about his new duties as serenely as if he had been on land. Therefore they found no opportunity to offer him the remedy they were wont to hand out to the usual run of shipmaster's apprentices—

"Just a wee drap o' saut water, And if a piece o' fat pork, after, Tied in a string ye tak' an' swallow, Ye'll find that muckle change will follow."

Nor did he have to listen to the suggestion, always gravely given, that the sufferer should make his will, which did not seem amiss, so awful are the pangs of that first hour when the novice is afraid he *will* die—and the second, when he is afraid he will *not*!

All in all, the Scotch lad stood that first short voyage to Whitehaven in fine shape. So bravely had he faced the jibes and rough play of the sailors coming across the Solway, so well had he performed his duties, that Mr. Younger's interest in him expanded. When they reached port he had the boy take quarters with him at his own splendid home, where Mrs. Younger treated him with as much consideration as if he were her own son. Here John stayed for almost two weeks, while the new vessel on which he was to sail was taking on her finishing touches and being fully provisioned. In the meantime he was not idle, running errands for his host and hostess, working in their garden, and making himself generally useful.

Spare moments he put in thumbing his way through various volumes in the splendid library of Mr. Younger. Indeed, so assiduously did he apply himself to reading several books on naval history that, the day he left, the ship-owner presented him with two such works, much to John's gratification. With his own meager savings he purchased an oilcloth wrapper for these treasures and stored them carefully away aboard the *Friendship*, the new vessel.

Mr. Younger's line of ships were engaged largely in the American trade; so when John learned that the *Friendship* was going to make her maiden voyage to Virginia, the very State in which his brother Willie was located, his joy knew no bounds. Just before he stepped aboard for the last time he mailed a letter to his mother, telling her of the happy tidings, and as the big ship worked out into the Irish Sea, with her bow pointed for the New Country across the Atlantic, he looked forward to the trip with a rare eagerness.

His ship was commanded by Captain Benson. This skipper was a stern disciplinarian, none too well liked by the crew. Yet he was kind to the young apprentice, who found him just in every particular, and admired his high-spirited nature, so much like his own.

The lad learned fast. With the sailors he was always a favorite. Before the vessel reached American waters he could climb a mast or yardarm with the most nimble of them, and was as fearless as the captain himself when the waves were running high.

At last the green shores of America were sighted one morning by the lookout at the masthead. Near sunset the *Friendship* dropped anchor in the quiet waters of the Rappahannock River, not far from the plantation where Willie Paul lived with William Jones, the cousin who had adopted him years ago.

Johnnie's heart beat like a trip-hammer as he made his way, after some inquiries, up the winding drive which led toward a big white house. All around stretched acres of fertile fields, now heavy with ripening grain and tobacco. At the rear of the great house were numbers of smaller buildings, about some of which he could see negro children playing. Surely *all* of this could not belong to the Jones estate! Why it was bigger than the wonderful premises of the Craiks!—even bigger than all of the fishing-village of Arbigland itself! The Scotch boy faltered. He stopped. He must have made a mistake. Once more he swept his eyes around at the huge fields, from one quarter of which came faintly rolling toward him the sounds of a rollicking negro chorus.

Just then a tall figure—that of a young man—appeared on the portico of the great house. This person gazed intently toward the lad, then proceeded in his direction.

As the young man came closer, John saw that he was a splendid-looking fellow. While slender he had a broad chest and square shoulders, and a heavy mass of wavy auburn hair crowned his bare head, behind which it was gathered in the manner of the period. Finer breeches, waistcoat, stockings, gaiters, and shoes, the boy had never seen.

The young man's blue eyes looked down into John's pleasantly and inquiringly. "Well, my lad," said he in perfect English, "can I serve you in any manner?"

"Sir," replied John awkwardly, "I fear I ha' been trespassing a wee bit. I ha' just come this day in a gude vessel, the *Friendship*, all the way from Whitehaven, England, and I am bent on seeing my brither who has lived some'r' in these parts this many a year."

"Your speech shows you to be Scotch. What is this brother's name?" asked the planter quickly.

"Willie Paul it was, but now it be Willie Jones because——"

"Willie Jones! And you are...?"

"Johnnie Paul, sir."

"Johnnie," said the young man, seizing him by the shoulders and squaring him around, as he peered earnestly down at the boy, "look fairly into my face. Tell me—is there anything you see there which reminds you of anybody you know?"

"On'y two things, sir. Ye ha'—asking pardon—the big ears o' my faither an' the twinklin' blue eyes o' my mither."

The young man smiled. Those blue eyes twinkled more than ever. "Johnnie Paul," cried he, "you are very observing; but apparently not enough so to recognize me as your brother!"

The next moment his big arms had swept around the little sailor, and Johnnie had never known such a happy moment. He was overjoyed to meet finally this brother he had never seen before. Together the happy pair went up the path and into the great house where the lad from far-away shores was made the welcome guest of the plantation owner and foster-father of Willie, William Jones himself.

Just two weeks the *Friendship* lay in the river discharging her consignment of farm implements, so much needed by the new settlers, for a cargo of tobacco and cotton to be taken back to England. Young John's services were not required aboard ship during this time, and it gave him a fine chance to visit with his brother and gain some knowledge of plantation life. He found that William Paul Jones had married since the family in Scotland had heard from him last, and that he was now overseer of his foster-father's estate, with a splendid future apparently awaiting him.

The premises boasted of some of the finest horses in the country. It was John's delight to mount one of these mettlesome animals and with his brother or Mr. Jones go cantering down the shady Virginia roads in the neighborhood, or, at slower pace, cover the grounds of the big plantation. Of an evening they would call on neighbors, else neighbors would partake of the hospitality of the Jones's. The boy took an immediate liking to the generous, outspoken class of people he met. The American boys especially pleased him. In their active, fearless play, and love for adventure, they seemed a part of his own bold and hardy Scotch spirit. Many a wrestling bout did he indulge in with the best of them, and while he was sometimes thrown he had the satisfaction of knowing that it never was by a chap younger than himself.

Mr. Jones took a strong fancy to the little Scotchman. Since Willie had been adopted he had come to regard the elder brother with the strongest of paternal affection, but now that he had grown up and married, the foster-father found himself yearning once more for young companionship. Just before Johnnie left, this kind-hearted planter offered to adopt him also. But the lad's real love was for the sea. Much as he liked this interesting, free life in Virginia, he did not feel that he could give up his precious ships for it.

So off he sailed for Whitehaven.

III

THE YOUNG SAILOR

Life before the mast in 1759 was a hard routine, not calculated to make a "sissy" or a mollycoddle out of any boy. Colleges and training-schools for turning out ship's officers there were none; every single man who attained such executive positions did so at the long and laborious expense of time and actual service in positions lower down the ladder.

Johnnie Paul knew all the hard work that lay before him, before he had been aboard the *Friendship* a fortnight, for there were many old veterans of the crew—failures themselves in the way of promotion—who were only too glad to try to discourage the lad because they felt irritated at their own lack of progress. One of the most persistent of these was a black-browed, bewhiskered fellow named Tom Whiddon. Whiddon was a jealous-minded sailor, given to sulky spells, and he seemed to take pleasure in telling John at every opportunity that the life of a sailor was a dog's life at the best, and that only men of money having a "pull" with the owners could ever hope to get an officer's berth.

The Scotch lad listened to Tom Whiddon's growling complaints with growing impatience, although politely enough at first. As the seaman continued to harass him he asked him to desist, but this only caused a coarse laugh from Whiddon and some of his associates who were disgruntled at Captain Benson's apparent liking for the young apprentice.

Finally came a day when the good ship lay becalmed. At such times a crew usually has difficulty to while away the hours. Between the times when they are "whistling for a wind" there is little to do except to talk, tell yarns, do stunts, and play practical jokes on one another.

John had already found out to his sorrow, by reason of several other becalmings on the trip from Whitehaven to America, that when there is a boy aboard, that boy is likely to be the chief butt of such practical jokes. As then it was so now. But as then he also now good-naturedly laughed with them at the pranks they played at his expense. It was only when Tom Whiddon, with a malicious grin on his face, publicly called him the "cap'n's baby" that Johnnie's quick Scotch temper got the best of him.

Like a flash he stood before the black-browed Whiddon, a belaying-pin in one hand, his hazel eyes snapping fire, his cheeks burning at the injustice of the remark.

"Say that again, Tom Whiddon, an' I'll knock ye flat on this deck!" cried Johnnie.

There was a tenseness in his tones, an earnestness in his demeanor that should have warned Whiddon. But the big bully saw only his own gigantic proportions as compared with the small bundle of quivering flesh confronting him. Stung by the lad's threat and the amused looks his comrades cast in his direction, Whiddon blurted out:

"Hi say it ag'in—'cap'n's baby'! an' hif you don't——"

The sailor was about to say, "Hif you don't drop that belayin'-pin Hi'll trounce you good an' proper, ye little snapper," when the boy's arm whipped forward, the belaying-pin landed on Whiddon's thick skull and he measured his length on the deck.

The crew had not looked for such summary action on the part of the master's-boy no more than had the burly Whiddon himself. It had seemed ridiculous to think such a small boy would go to such extremes in upholding his honor and dignity. Now, as they gazed down aghast at their fallen comrade, who moved not a muscle, they were almost as stunned as he.

When they awoke, one or two of them sprang forward and seized the boy, but a half-dozen others, including the first and second mates, pulled them away.

"Leave the lad alone!" they demanded. "Whiddon got no more than he deserved."

This seemed to be the consensus of opinion. The fellow was deservedly unpopular. Not a hand was lifted for his relief until young John Paul himself got some water, sprinkled it in his face, and brought him to. This tenderness of heart was characteristic of the lad in later years. It is said that when he became skipper of his own vessel, on more than one occasion his hot temper caused him to cuff or kick one of his officers for a breach of discipline, while his sympathetic nature immediately afterward prompted him to invite the culprit to mess with him in his cabin.

Merchant ships then plying for trade were not fitted out with the refinements of a modern hotel, as might be said of many of them nowadays; after a few days out even the captain's table could not boast fresh provisions, and long voyages almost inevitably ended with scurvy among the crew, due to lack of green vegetables and an overdose of brine. Though the *menu* lacked variety, the same could not be said of the names of the dishes which were not only picturesque but in some cases actually descriptive. For instance, there was "Salt Junk and Pork," "Lobscouse,"

"Plum-duff," "Dog's Body," "Sea Pies," "Rice Tail," "Hurryhush," "Pea Coffee," and "Bellywash."

With our steam and wireless to-day it is hard to realize the complete isolation which was formerly the seaman's lot. Empires might rise and fall, and Jack be none the wiser until he touched at port, or spoke some swifter craft within hail of the skipper's brazen-throated speaking-trumpet. Often becalmed for days at a time, in the manner previously referred to, with nothing to break the sameness of glassy water and nebulous horizon, the most trifling incident furnished food for conversation and attention.

Even when the ship was under headway, the incessant moaning and whistling of wind through the rigging, the dull flapping of canvas at every shift of the breeze, itself bore a sense of monotony which made the crew long for the sight of a friendly sail or a bit of land. Once in port, the captain, relieved of responsibility, had his own affairs to occupy him ashore, as did most of his officers. His crew, divided between land and craft alternately, were entertained aboard by scores of natives with baskets of gewgaws to sell, and very often guzzled rum ashore until they could scarcely zig-zag their way back to the yawl.

Despite its temptations, life at sea had a broadening influence for the average young man of the time. He returned very much more the man of the world, with harder muscles, and was far better able to take care of himself than his stay-at-home brother. On his voyages he gathered a store of extensive and varied information relating to the races and the geography of the world, that he could never get out of books. True, his associations and experiences made him a rough, blunt-spoken fellow as a rule; but on the whole they made his heart more sympathetic for those in trouble, more understanding of the big things in life.

Johnnie Paul was now an attractive lad, high-spirited, quick to anger at injustice, open and honorable,—traits he seemed to have taken from the Highland blood of his mother. To his father, the Lowlander, he probably owed his restraining sense of strategy and caution. But for the latter inheritance of character it is likely his bold spirit would often have gotten him into trouble, and he could never have won the fights which he did later on. While John's rough life, in association with common seamen from the time that he was twelve years old, and his lack of previous education, made difficult his becoming what he ardently wished to be—a cultivated gentleman—he applied himself diligently to that end. During the long years on the deep which followed, by hard study the boy educated himself to a considerable degree, not only in seamanship and navigation, but also in naval history and in the French and Spanish languages. On a voyage his habit was to seek out a quiet spot, with his books, at every lull in his tasks.

On shore, instead of carousing with his associates, he was given to hunting out the most distinguished or best-informed person he could find; by chatting with him, he added to his rapidly increasing fund of knowledge. His handwriting was always the painful scrawl of a schoolboy, probably because being far more adept with his tongue than with his spelling, he preferred to dictate most of his letters, that their recipients should not suspect his limited schooling, a matter about which he was always very sensitive.

For four years following his maiden voyage, John Paul was a member of the crew of the *Friendship*. His voyages were mainly to and from the West Indies. During this time he managed to call twice upon his brother Willie in Virginia, and each time the people there grew to like him better, and he to appreciate the attractions of the New Country. He also had been to see his folks at Arbigland once or twice, on occasions when his ship was laying-over at Whitehaven, and these were happy occasions for all concerned, as we may suppose.

John's rise in the merchant service was rapid. When he was sixteen, a sturdy youth with the nimbleness of a cat and almost the strength of a man, Mr. Younger retired from business, and as a reward to the capability and faithfulness of his charge, the ship-owner returned him the indentures which made him his own master. In addition to this he presented him to the captain of the *King George* of Whitehaven, a slaver, with recommendation that the lad be given an appointment as first-mate.

It must be remembered that at this time the slave-trade was not regarded as anything dishonorable. Numerous vessels were attracted to it as a money-making venture, and openly plied back and forth between the home of the black man and the island of Jamaica. Few sailors, few officers, few of the people at large, thought it wrong to steal lusty young negroes and negresses away from their parents and kinsmen and offer them for sale to the Jamaican slave-dealers and plantation owners.

So young John Paul first engaged in the trade without any compunctions of conscience. But it was not for long. At the end of two years he had seen so many broken hearts among the blacks as a result of the forced partings, had been an observer of so much unnecessary suffering because of the cruelty of the rough fellows who handled the human freight, that his heart sickened. In fact, so disgusted was he that he even sold out the sixth interest which he had obtained in the ship, quitted it, and boarded the *John O'Gaunt*, at Kingston, Jamaica, bound as a passenger for Whitehaven.

On the trip home the captain, mate, and all but five of the crew of the *John O'Gaunt* died of yellow fever. Not a man was left, except John Paul, who knew enough about navigation to bring the afflicted ship into port. So the lad took charge. With neatness and dispatch he guided the brig across the dangerous waters of the Atlantic and into her haven. Her pleased owners rewarded him with a share of her cargo, and gratified him even more by making him captain and supercargo of a new ship—the *John*—which was engaged in the West Indian merchant trade.

Life on a merchantman is rough enough to-day; it was far rougher at that time. To maintain discipline at sea required a strong hand and a tongue none too gentle. Kind-hearted enough by nature, John had learned his lessons by this time; he knew that indecision and softness had no place in an efficient skipper's makeup before his men, and while good enough to his crew at all times he insisted that they obey his commands with respect and promptness.

During the third voyage of the *John*, when fever had greatly reduced the crew and every man on board was more or less fretful and irritable, Mungo Maxwell, a mulatto carpenter, became mutinous to such an extent that the young commander deemed it advisable to have him flogged, not only as fitting punishment, but as a salutary example for the observation of the remainder of the crew. The chastisement duly took place. It was not unusually severe, but it happened that, unknown to the youth, the man was just coming down himself with the scourge. He took to his bed, the fever gripped him, and he never arose again.

A few envious enemies of John immediately circulated reports that the mulatto had been struck down and murdered by the young captain. He was arrested by the governor of Tobago, in the vicinity of which the vessel happened to be at the time, and taken before the tribunal of that place. Since the body of the stricken carpenter had been immediately consigned to the deep, following the custom in such deaths, it could not be produced to substantiate John's claims of innocence, but witnesses in his favor were plentiful enough to aid in his acquittal.

This incident, in spite of its outcome, worried the lad a great deal. His pride was hurt. In a letter to his mother and sisters, he referred frequently to it with remorse, and in those parts where he told of people still throwing it up to him in a condemning manner, his language was even bitter. Can we blame him?

A year later, in 1870, when he was twenty, John learned that William Jones, foster-father of his brother, had died, bequeathing to Willie his entire property of three thousand acres, the buildings, animals, slaves, and a sloop. A clause of the will particularly personal was to the effect that, should the adopted son die without children, the estate, excepting an adequate provision for Willie's wife, was to go to his youngest brother, our John Paul.

The next two years the young captain continued to guide the *Two Friends*, of Kingston, Jamaica, of which he had taken command some four years earlier. Numerous voyages were made to the Indian Ocean, and cargoes of woolen and thread goods brought back. Twice trips were made to Baltic ports.

Finally, in 1771, John obtained command of the *Betsy*, of London, a ship trading with the West Indies. This venture made it possible for the young man to save a considerable amount of money, a goodly share of which he fondly anticipated sending home to his mother and sisters.

Just a year later, in 1772, business having called him in that vicinity, he ran the *Betsy* into the Rappahannock. He had not seen or heard from Willie for over a year. This would be a splendid opportunity. How surprised his brother would be!

At the door he was met by a servant who knew him at first sight. The negro's eyes danced with delight, his mouth spread into a broad grin, showing two rows of glistening white teeth. But the next moment he grew very sober.

"Hush, Marse John," he said in the lowest of whispers. "Ah's suah sorry t' tell yo', but Marse Willyum am berry, berry sick."

Going in quickly, the young sailor was grief-stricken to find his brother lying at the point of death.

IV

THE YOUNG PLANTER

William Jones was, indeed, too ill to recognize his brother, and died in that condition. John felt the blow keenly, the more so because he could not have a last word with the kinsman he had seen so little of, and had come to regard with such strong affection.

In accordance with the provisions of the will, the bulk of the estate was now due to go to Johnnie Paul, provided the latter would accept Jones as a surname. Our young sailor, after some deliberation, decided to make the change, settle down, and become a Virginia planter. But he could not satisfy himself with dropping the name of Paul. This was a family heirloom which he felt he must preserve, especially now since he was the only male member of his immediate family possessing it, his good father having gone some months before. Therefore, he forthwith discarded his Christian name of John—whose commonplaceness he had never liked—and became known as Paul Jones. Under this half-assumed appellation he did the really big things of his career which brought him fame. Under it he shouldered responsibilities of which any true-hearted, loyal American citizen might well be proud, although he was only the son of a poor Scotch gardener, a young man without education, without a country he could really claim as his own.

Paul Jones—as we shall now have to call him—found that he had inherited "3000 acres of prime land, bordering for twelve furlongs on the right bank of the Rappahannock, running back southward three miles, 1000 acres of which are cleared and under plough or grass, 2000 acres of which are strong first-growth timber; a grist-mill with flour-cloth and fans turned by water power; mansion, overseer's house, negro quarters, stables, tobacco houses, threshing-floor, river-wharf, one sloop of twenty tons, thirty negroes of all ages (eighteen adults), twenty horses and colts, eighty neat cattle and calves, sundry sheep and swine; and all necessary means of tilling the soil."

With the property came also old Duncan Macbean. This canny, tough old Scotsman Willie Jones had saved from the tomahawks of the Indians at the time of Braddock's rout. He had brought him home, nursed him until well of his wounds, and then made him overseer of the plantation. In this capacity Duncan had amply proved his efficiency. He had become greatly attached to the place, and in his will the master had requested that he be continued as overseer as long as he was physically and mentally capable.

Paul Jones sent the *Betsy* back to London under the command of his first-mate, with word to her owners that, for the present at least, he was relinquishing the attractions of the sea. He then settled down in earnest to the new life that had opened up before him.

As in everything he undertook, he waded into the duties confronting him with an interest keen and thorough. He was not afraid to ask questions of those whose experience warranted them knowing more than he about his new task, no matter how humble or high their stations. In this way he learned the tricks of the planter with surprising rapidity. It was not long before he saw the advisability of rotating his tobacco crops with sowings of maize, that the fertility of his fields might not be exhausted, and a number of neighboring planters who had never thought of such a thing before, followed suit.

There was not a horse on the plantation, nor in the county which could unseat him. So much was he liked by his slaves that they anticipated his every wish, it seemed. In the early day, before the sun had become intolerable, he rode over his broad acres at a leisurely pace, noting the crops, the black workers, the pickaninnies at play,—everything. Apparently nothing tending toward a betterment of the condition of his help and the acres they tilled seemed to escape him. A gentle bit of censure here, a pat on a woolly head there, a trinket in a child's outstretched dusky hand, and he would turn his horse's head in another direction.

The surrounding forests contained game in profusion; and the low sandy marshes around Urbana abounded in great flocks of snipe and other water-fowl. With old Duncan Macbean the young master often shouldered the fine Lancaster rifle left by his brother, stuck a brace of pistols in his belt, and spent a day in the wilds. No better shot than the old Scotsman could be found in the whole country. Although an old Indian wound had left him lame, this in no wise interfered with his wonderful skill with either pistol or rifle. He could shoot from either hand or either shoulder, from almost any position, and put a ball through a wild turkey's head at a hundred yards.

Paul Jones could scarcely credit the evidence of his eyes when he first saw old Duncan shoot, for he had never seen such accuracy before. An intense desire came over him to master firearms with equal skill. He imparted this wish to his overseer, and the consequence was that in the course of the next two years the old veteran taught him to handle the pistol and rifle with a deadliness which became the talk of the countryside.

However, the ability to shoot was really more a matter of necessity than an accomplishment in those days. Scattering bands of the Rappahannock Indians often stole down stream to the holdings of the Scotch-Irish planters along the tidewater shores, and when opportunity offered, ran off portions of their live stock, or even sent a wicked arrow through an unwary white man. In her scrolled coach, creaking and swaying on its great hinges and leather straps, milady never took her airings down the rough sandy roads without a guarding retinue of armed slaves and whites. Nor did men themselves venture forth in the fastnesses without their fingers playing about hammer and trigger, ever ready to throw up the former at the slightest suspicious sight or sound, ready to pull the latter when they became convinced that such a procedure was warranted.

Young Paul Jones enjoyed his new life to the utmost. The constant peril from the redskins, the exciting brushes which he and old Duncan Macbean had with some of them on different occasions, the thrilling hunts in the forest, all went to satisfy his active, adventure-loving nature. On the other hand, he had plenty of spare time in which to gratify his ambitions for study, for becoming a man of power in his own section as well as in the affairs of the new nation. He continued to study from books, perfected his knowledge of the French and Spanish languages, and even traveled over the Colonies quite extensively. He entertained lavishly at home. His gallantry and courtesy made him very popular.

In his trips away from home he met many prominent statesmen of the time, and renewed friendships with others whom he had previously met. Among the latter was Joseph Hewes, with whom he was unusually intimate. Other noted men of his acquaintance were Thomas Jefferson, Philip Livingston, George Washington, Benjamin Franklin, the Lees, and Robert and Gouverneur Morris.

For some time the Colonists had been growing more and more restless under the burdensome taxes and conditions imposed upon them by England, the mother-country. The governors she appointed seemed to deal with the people unjustly, even cruelly at times. Protests did no good. If one official was removed a worse one was put in his place. So life in the new land, instead of flourishing, became a burden.

Bitterness began to creep into the voices of the Colonists when they talked of Great Britain. The man who thought conditions all right was frowned upon by the majority and called a "Tory." He was told either to keep his silence, or go back across the seas. The majority—the "Whigs"—did not want such men howling for the king on the virgin ground which they had come hundreds of miles to settle and keep free from the fetters of aristocratic rulers and their smothering taxes.

In 1774, Paul Jones, then twenty-seven years of age, returning from Edmonton, stopped over in Norfolk to visit some friends. Several British ships lay at anchor in the harbor. The Colonists forgot their grievances under the impulse of their natural hospitality. Wishing to show kindness to the king's sailors rather than loyalty to his empire, the Americans entertained the officers at an elaborate ball.

As customary at such functions wine was furnished. Instead of partaking of this sparingly, most of the young English officers drank freely, and became very insolent and abusive. Stepping up to one of the most talkative of them—Lieutenant Parker, by name—Paul Jones demanded:

"Did I not overhear you say, sir, that in the case of a revolt in this country England will easily suppress it?"

"Thash jus' what I said," replied Lieutenant Parker thickly. "Mean it too, m'lad. But I might add that if the courage of your men ish no finer'n the virtue of your women, you'll be licked before the fight's one day old."

In an instant the fist of the young planter, as hard as an oak knot beneath its laced cuff, swung out from his broad shoulder. The British officer went down like a log.

At once there was an aggressive movement on the part of his comrades; but the Americans, now thoroughly aroused to the defense of their ideals, flocked around Paul Jones in such numbers that the king's men fell back, picked up their helpless companion, and hurried aboard their ships.

Expecting that, after the custom of the day, Lieutenant Parker might challenge him to a duel, Paul Jones at once proceeded to make arrangements with a friend, Mr. Granville Hurst, to represent him in the event of any negotiations.

"Propose pistols at ten paces," said the young planter. "Advise the gentleman I will meet him at Craney Island, at such time as he may desire."

But this meeting never took place, for the very good reason that Lieutenant Parker heard about Paul Jones's unerring use of a pistol; his sloop departed at ebb tide for Charlestown, and, so far as he was concerned personally, the incident seemed closed.

The Colonists, however, did not forget it in a hurry. Like wildfire the news of the encounter spread. Colonial newspapers all gave considerable space to it. Suddenly Paul Jones found himself the most-talked-of man in Virginia. He was the hero of men, women, and children. Unofficially he had struck the first blow of the threatening conflict with England.

V

THE BIRTH OF THE UNITED STATES NAVY

The following spring—that of 1775—Paul Jones decided to board his sloop and make a little pleasure trip by sea to Boston. With his crew and two favorite slaves, Cato and Scipio, he sailed down the river, worked out into the Atlantic, and keeping close to the New Jersey headlands, pointed north.

When he reached New York he dropped anchor, intending to meet some of his friends in that city. One of the very first of these he encountered was William Livingston. This patriot's face showed plenty of excitement. "Paul, have you heard the news?" he asked.

"I have not been favored," replied Paul Jones. "I trust it is nothing serious concerning your own family."

"I fear it *is* serious; but it concerns my family no more than it concerns any other family in the Colonies," was William Livingston's answer. "Paul, my friend, the British have beaten us at Lexington!"

Paul Jones was gravely concerned. He plied his friend with many questions. After a long discussion they parted. The young planter immediately gave up his plans for visiting Boston; he wished to go home and in the seclusion of the plantation calmly think over the matter and decide what to do.

Within twenty-four hours after his arrival he sent to Thomas Jefferson the following letter:

> "It is, I think, to be taken for granted that there can be no more temporizing. I am too recently from the mother country, and my knowledge of the temper of the king, his ministers, and their majority in the House of Commons, is too fresh to allow me to believe that anything is, or possibly can be in store except either war to the knife or total submission to complete slavery.
>
> "... I cannot conceive of submission to complete slavery; therefore only war is in sight. The Congress, therefore, must soon meet again, and when it meets it must face the necessity of taking those measures which it did not take last fall in its first session, namely, provision for armament by land and sea.

"Such being clearly the position of affairs, I beg you to keep my name in your memory when the Congress shall assemble again, and in any provision that may be taken for a naval force, to call upon me in any capacity which your knowledge of my seafaring experience and your opinions of my qualifications may dictate."

One morning, a short time after this, Paul Jones received word that two French frigates had come to anchor in Hampton Roads. With the hospitality of the true sailor and true Virginia planter he loaded his sloop with the best green vegetables the plantation afforded, and started down the Rappahannock to welcome the newcomers.

The two frigates were in command of Captain De Kersaint, one of the ablest officers in the French navy, who afterwards became an admiral. The second in command was no less than the Duc De Chartres, eldest son of the Duc D'Orléans, who had sent De Chartres to America on a "cruise of instruction," to fit him for the hereditary post of Lord High Admiral of France. He was Paul Jones's own age exactly, and with his charming wife, the Duchesse De Chartres, he received the young planter with a great cordiality. Their liking for Paul Jones increased as they chatted. In fact, the Duke himself took such a violent fancy to their guest that when the latter asked if he might be shown plans of the construction of their splendid frigate. *La Terpischore*, with a view to offering suggestions to the Colonists in building war craft, the French nobleman readily assented. With royal prerogative he ordered his ship's carpenter to make deck and sail drawings, hull details,—everything that could in any way aid the young Scotchman in understanding the essential constructive features of the vessel.

It was of inestimable advantage to Paul Jones to have had the opportunity of inspecting at such close range, much less get drawings of, one of the best and most modern ships of the French navy. It is not strange that the American frigate *Alliance*, built some time later, followed closely the same general lines as *La Terpischore*; that she mounted the same battery—twenty-eight long 12-pounders on the gun deck, and ten long 9-pounders above. Was this merely a coincidence? Or, on the other hand, did the young Scotchman have a hand in the matter?

At a meeting of the Continental Congress on May 10, 1775, the Naval Committee invited Paul Jones to lay before it such information and advice as might seem to him useful in assisting the committee in discharging its labors. Paul Jones felt strongly on the subject of establishing a navy, and thought that the only way to start was to offer prizes to the crews of privateersmen. In a letter to Joseph Hewes he observed:

"If our enemies, with the best established and most formidable navy in the universe, have found it expedient to assign all prizes to the captors, how much more is such policy essential to our infant fleet? But I need no argument to convince you of the necessity of making the emoluments of our navy equal, if not superior, to theirs."

In this appeal to Congress there was good common-sense. Paul Jones was not actuated by a love of gain; he was in the struggle because he thought it a righteous cause. Yet he knew that while he had the profits of his plantation for the past two or three seasons—some 4000 pounds—to fall back upon when his Government allowances should fail to meet expenses, the average Colonist did not. The wives and children of the latter must be fed and clothed while he was away fighting. Unless he could be promised ample revenue from prizes, Paul Jones knew that Jack would fight half-heartedly and in the dumps, even though he loved his country in every fiber of his being. His pitifully inadequate Government allowance of eight dollars a month was surely no attraction.

On November 15, 1776, Congress improved this situation somewhat, but did not meet Paul Jones's wishes in the matter, by resolving "that a bounty of twenty dollars be paid to the commanders, officers, and men, of such Continental ships or vessels of war as shall make a prize of any British ships or vessels of war, for every cannon on board such a prize at the time of such capture; and eight dollars per head for every man then on board and belonging to such prize."

In addition to this General Washington approved the following distribution of the prize: "That the captain or commander should receive six shares; the first-lieutenant, five, the second-lieutenant and the surgeon, four; the master, three; steward, two; mate, gunner, gunner's-mate, boatswain, and sergeant, one and one-half shares; the private, one share." Nothing was said about the poor cook. Undoubtedly he ranked with the ordinary seaman when the time of distribution came.

To all intents and purposes an American, the truth remains that Paul Jones was a Scotchman. His enthusiastic soul was wholly for the cause of liberty in his new country, but the men who envied him and wanted the offices for which his high capabilities fitted him so signally never let him and others forget that he was an alien. This was, of course, quite absurd; for what were they themselves? What had they been until a few months ago? The fact is, Paul Jones had served under three masters, until he was a far more competent officer than many of those in the established navies of Europe, where influence and patronage often made officers of men of long lineage and short experience.

Thus in the *Journal of Congress*, dated December 22, 1775, the name of Paul Jones heads the list of first-lieutenants, instead of the list of captains as it should. His friend Joseph Hewes, who championed the candidates from the southern colonies, had done his best to make the young planter a captain, but had failed at the antagonism of John Adams, who represented the candidates from the northern colonies, which demanded full control of naval affairs.

When affairs had at last been worked down to a point of action by sea, the nucleus of the first navy of the new country consisted of the *Alfred*, the *Columbus*, the *Andrew Doria*, the *Providence*, and the *Cabot*. Five little ships to face the finely-appointed scores of frigates and sloops-of-war in the service of the king!

VI

RAISING THE FIRST AMERICAN FLAG

That winter of 1776 was a cold one. Snow had lain heavy in the streets of Philadelphia since frigid blasts had brought the first downfall in December. In January, the Delaware River, like every other stream in the country, was locked in the grip of ice, ice a foot or more in thickness. It was only by the constant plying up and down stream of a couple of sturdy whaling-ships, equipped with steel-jacketed bows, that an open channel could be maintained in the Delaware for the passage of ordinary wooden-hulled craft.

Along the waterfront of the city innumerable masts and spars made a somber network against the dull blue of the winter sky. On board some of the larger of the vessels, despite the cold, men were at work repairing and overhauling. Well down the glittering sea of ice a group of five ships swung at anchor in the channel. Their decks, too, were a scene of action.

All of this was taken in with a few swift glances by a quick-stepping, stalwart young man who came down to the wharf and paused to look about him. He was a comely-looking fellow, with broad shoulders, and a face as bronzed as a South Sea Islander's.

It was the young Scotchman and planter, Paul Jones. But his immaculate linen had been discarded. In its place he appeared in the trim uniform of a Continental marine lieutenant—blue coat with red-bound button-holes, round-cuffed blue breeches, and black gaiters.

As he looked about for a boat to take him out to the five ships riding at anchor, Paul Jones's eye fell on a tall, lithe young man who was just in the act of tying the painter of a whaler's yawl to one of the wharf timbers.

Paul Jones stepped briskly up to him. "Pardon me, my fine fellow," he said, "but a guinea is yours if you will row me out to the larger of yon vessels, the *Alfred*, where I am in urgent service."

The young man wheeled around, displaying features unmistakably those of an Indian, but of an unusually intelligent composition. His coal-black eyes swept over his questioner. "I, Wannashego, will take the white sea-soldier," he replied in excellent English.

Without further ado, Paul Jones sprang nimbly down into the boat. Its owner cast loose and followed.

As his companion pulled lustily away in the direction of the American ships, Paul Jones sat studying the rower. When and where had this redskin of the American forest picked up such splendid address? What marvelous trick of fate had possessed him of such skill with the white man's oars?

"You are an Indian, are you not?" inquired the lieutenant presently.

"An Indian of Narragansett tribe," was the proud reply.

"Where did you learn to handle a boat in this manner?"

"On whaling cruises, sir."

"You belong to one of these whaling-ships at the wharves, then?"

"Yes, sir; to *Walrus*. She lies upstream a bit, sir. Three years I have been with her."

"How is it you came to leave your people, Wannashego?" asked Paul Jones curiously.

"My father, Tassa-menna-tayka, a chief who loves the white people, he sent me from near Martha's Vineyard to learn your ways and be like you," declared the young Indian. There was a short pause; he turned his head for a moment to take his bearings, and then continued: "Sir, I ask if yonder ships are to fight the great country across the sea?"

"They are, Wannashego."

"You goin' to fight on 'em?"

"I expect to."

"I like to fight on 'em, too," was the sententious rejoinder of the young redskin.

"Do you mean that?" asked Paul Jones sharply. "If you do, Wannashego, I think I can get Captain Saltonstall, of my ship, the *Alfred*, to ship you, as we are short-handed."

"Mean it a heap," said the Indian. "I shoot good. Make two bangs—get two Red-coats."

Paul Jones laughed. "I hope so. Well, Wannashego, I'll see what I can do for you."

Shortly the boat's nose touched the accommodation-ladder over the *Alfred's* side. The young lieutenant held out the promised guinea to Wannashego, but the Indian straightened up proudly. "I don't want money," said he. "I like America country heap much. You fight for him, so I help you beat our enemies, the Red-coats."

It was a crude expression of sentiment, but Paul Jones interpreted it correctly, and was deeply affected by it. "Wannashego," he cried, "return to your captain. If he will release you, and you still want to fight the Red-coat soldiers of the sea, come to me on this ship to-morrow and I will stir heaven and earth to make you a member of our crew."

Captain Saltonstall was to command the ship, but he had not yet arrived. So, for the present at least, upon Paul Jones rested the duty of preparing her for sea. Under his leadership, arrangements went on speedily and smoothly. The *Alfred* bid fair to be in readiness before some of her sister ships, it seemed.

Next morning, before the sun was an hour high, a yawl containing two men was seen approaching. At first the lieutenant thought it might be Captain Saltonstall himself, but his glass soon showed him his mistake. It was the young Narragansett Indian, Wannashego, who evidently had secured one of the sailors of his old ship to row him out to the *Alfred*.

Paul Jones made him welcome, telling him that he was quite sure the captain would make no objection when he should appear. Thus Wannashego, the first and one of the very few full-blooded Indians to fight in the first navy of this country, became a tentative member of the *Alfred's* crew. He took hold of his duties happily and energetically, outdoing many of his white companions.

As for the temporary commander, from the time the foot of Paul Jones touched the deck of the vessel his active spirit pervaded everything, and the officers under him, as well as the men, felt the force of his executive power. Besides working all day, he and the other officers stood watch and watch on deck throughout the wintry nights, to prevent desertions; and although every other vessel in the squadron lost men in this manner, not a single deserter got away from the *Alfred*.

"An' I'll bet a herrin' ag'in a p'tater, mates," remarked Bill Putters, quartermaster, in the confidence of the forecastle, "that this Leftenant Jones is a real seaman wot could handle this yere ol' gal better'n Cap'n Saltonstall. I kin tell it by the cut o' his jib, the way he squares away to tackle any job he undertakes."

"Bet so, too, Bill," supported the bos'n, Tom Wilkerson; "an' I'll go you a cooky he's a fighter. He speaks to most of us so soft you might think his voice was a tune from a fiddle; but, by Johnny! when Pete Walker didn't do what he told him to, yes'dy, he thundered at him in a way that made poor Pete's head rattle with the jar, an' Pete perty nigh dislocated his spinal collum jumpin' to do what he wanted him to. *I'd* like to see the leftenant in full charge. If we ever met up with any o' them pets of the king you bet there would be some fur flyin'—an' it wouldn't be ours as much as theirs, neether!"

One day, in the midst of the bustle of fitting out the ship, Commodore Hopkins, who was to command the little squadron, came on board the *Alfred*. He was formally received at the gangway by Paul Jones and shown over the ship by him.

The commodore was a big, heavy-set man who had spent the best part of his life at sea. He examined the vessel carefully, but made no favorable comments, and the young lieutenant began to fear his work had displeased the senior officer.

But it turned out otherwise. A little later, standing on the quarter-deck, surrounded by the officers, Commodore Hopkins turned to Paul Jones and said:

"Your work pleases me extremely, and my confidence in you, sir, is such that if Captain Saltonstall should not appear by the time these ships are due to sail, I shall hoist my flag on this ship and give you command of her."

A flush of gratification arose in Paul Jones's dark face. He bowed with the graceful courtesy that always distinguished him. "Thank you, commodore," said he, "and may I be pardoned for expressing the hope that Captain Saltonstall may not arrive in time! And when your flag is hoisted on the *Alfred*, I trust there will be ready a flag of the United Colonies to fly at the peak-halyards. I aspire to be the first man to raise that flag upon the ocean!"

Commodore Hopkins smiled. "If the Congress is as slow as I expect it will be, some time will elapse before it will have adopted a flag; and there will not be time to have one made, much less, before we sail."

In this he was mistaken. The Congress had practically decided upon the flag, and quite certain of its selection, Paul Jones from his own pocket had already purchased the materials to make it. Bill Putters was an old sail-maker, therefore handy with a needle, which it was his boast he "could steer like a reg'lar tailor-man." To him the young lieutenant entrusted the making of the first official flag of America they had seen—a task which swelled old Bill up with a wonderful pride, as well it might.

One stormy February day, when the channel had been freed from ice enough for the little squadron to get out, the *Alfred* was ready to lend her spotless decks to the formality of the flag-raising. Captain Saltonstall had arrived some days before. This disappointed Paul Jones. But he was as ready to do his duty as first-lieutenant, as in the hoped-for higher office.

The commodore's boat was seen approaching on the chill waters of the river. The horizon was overcast. Dun clouds, driven by a strong wind, scurried across the troubled sky. The boatswain's call, "All hands to muster!" sounded through the ship. In a wonderfully short time, owing to the careful drilling of Paul Jones, the three hundred sailors and one hundred marines were drawn up on deck. The sailors, a fine-looking body of American seamen, were formed in ranks on the port side of the quarter-deck, while abaft of them stood the marine guard under arms. On the starboard side were the petty officers, and on the quarter-deck proper were the commissioned officers in full uniform, swords at their sides. Paul Jones headed this line.

When it was reported, "All hands up and aft!" Captain Saltonstall emerged out of the cabin. At this Paul Jones, having previously arranged it, called out, "Quartermaster!" and Bill Putters, perfectly groomed, stepped from the ranks of the petty officers and saluted.

In his hand, carefully rolled up, Bill carried a small bundle. Unrolling this he followed Paul Jones briskly aft to the flagstaff. He affixed the flag to the halyards, along with the broad pennant of a commodore just below, saw that the lines were free, and then stood at attention.

Meantime the commodore's boat had reached the ladder, and he came over the side. Just as his foot touched the quarter-deck the flag with the pennant, under Paul Jones's energetic hands, was hauled swiftly upward. At the top the breeze caught it in all its fullness, flung it free to the air, and the sun at that moment burst through the clouds which had enveloped it, and bathed the emblem in all its fresh glory.

Every officer from the commodore down instantly removed his cap in patriotic reverence. The drummer boys beat a double-ruffle. A tremendous cheer burst from the sailors and marines.

This was not the present well-known Stars-and-Stripes, which was evolved later, but the Pine-tree and Rattlesnake Flag with the motto, "Don't Tread On Me!" As an emblem it was not at all artistic; but the men who now saw it flung to the breeze for the first time thought only of the sentiment it expressed, a sentiment still paramount in the heart of every true-blooded American. And among those who so loudly cheered it no man was more enthusiastic than the young Narragansett Indian, Wannashego.

Commodore Hopkins advanced toward Lieutenant Paul Jones and said: "I congratulate you, sir, upon your enterprise. This flag was only adopted in Congress yesterday. You are the very first to fly it."

Within an hour the *Columbus*, the *Andrew Doria*, the *Cabot*, and the *Providence*, led by the *Alfred*, were making out toward the open sea under full spread of canvas, ready to meet whatsoever of the mighty foe that might appear.

VII

AN INGLORIOUS CRUISE

The first enterprise determined upon was an expedition to the island of New Providence, in the West Indies. As it had been learned that Fort Nassau was well supplied with powder and shot—munitions of war sadly wanting in the Colonies—it was thought a sudden descent might be profitable.

The moment the English sighted the little squadron, a warning gun was fired from the fort, and all haste made to remove and conceal as much of the powder as possible. Delayed in getting into the harbor by a sandbar at its mouth, further delayed by poor judgment on the part of Commodore Hopkins, it was some time before the smaller vessels could work their way in far enough to effect a landing of their marines.

Then it was only to find a small amount of arms and stores awaiting them. Chagrined at his ill success, the commodore carried off the governor of the island as a hostage.

Now all sail was set, and the American squadron made its way cautiously along the New England coast. Although every part of these waters was swarming with British vessels, it was determined to try to gain an entrance into Long Island Sound by way of Narragansett Bay.

Paul Jones went about his arduous duties as first-lieutenant of the *Alfred* with his customary energy and determination. But at heart he cherished a secret dissatisfaction. Coupled with his disappointment at his own low official station was a growing impression that the senior officer of the squadron, Commodore Hopkins himself, was incompetent. In a number of instances during the Providence Island operation, the keen eyes of the first-lieutenant had caught him in blunders. Although the commodore might prove brave enough in an encounter, Paul Jones was sure that he was not above the average in either enterprise or intelligence. At the outset of the expedition the young officer was wild to meet the enemy, regardless of numbers. Now, with a grave doubt gripping his heart, he feared that they might meet Commodore Wallace's British fleet off Newport.

But the day passed without adventure. Numerous white sails were seen in the distance, none of which drew any nearer. Commodore Hopkins, being well weighted down with the cannon and supplies captured at New Providence, made no effort to investigate these far-off ships. "It is well to let sleeping dogs lie," he said when Captain Saltonstall proposed going after them.

Paul Jones's intrepid heart was sickened at such display of indifference. With his capacity for meeting extraordinary dangers with extraordinary resources of mind and courage, he could only despise the risks that other men shunned.

The young Narragansett Indian, who had been appointed boatswain's mate by Captain Saltonstall, was also clearly disgruntled at the commodore's weak attitude. But beyond muttering impatiently under his breath when he heard Commodore Hopkins's remarks about "sleeping dogs," and nudging Paul Jones, with flashing black eyes, Wannashego was discreet enough to say nothing. Intuitively the brave redskin knew that his Scotch friend felt as he did.

Toward night they entered the blue waters of Narragansett Bay. A young moon hung trembling in the heavens. The sky was cloudless, and the stars shone brilliantly. Wannashego slipped noiselessly up to where Paul Jones stood on the after-deck. The Indian youth pointed down to the gurgling green swells as they swept aft along the *Alfred's* hull. "These are the waters of my people, the Narragansetts," he said softly. "They touch the land of my old home and playgrounds."

"Wannashego, do you wish to go back to your people?" asked Paul Jones curiously.

He shook his black-locked head. "No," he answered—"if I can fight Red-coat sea soldiers soon. But if I have to run away when see 'em, like this, I like to go back an' ketchum whale on whaler-ship ag'in." He ended with an expressive grunt of disgust, and took himself off as silently as he had appeared.

Shortly after this—about midnight—the lookout on the *Alfred's* quarter made out Block Island. It seemed that his call had hardly died away when a cry of "Sail ho!" was heard from the direction of the *Cabot*.

With his night-glass to his eye Commodore Hopkins saw, about a half-mile away, the shadowy form of a ship. Captain Saltonstall also took a look at her. Several conjectures were raised as to her identity, and then the glass was handed to the first-lieutenant.

"What do you think she is, Mr. Jones?" asked Commodore Hopkins. He had more confidence in Paul Jones than he dared to confess, even to himself.

"I should say she was a British frigate, sir," was the lieutenant's prompt reply. "She is too small for a ship-of-the-line, and she does not carry sail enough for a merchantman under this breeze. It would seem to me that she is merely cruising about on the lookout for somebody."

"That 'somebody' is probably ourselves," answered the commodore uneasily, "if she's a British frigate as you think. She's likely out on scout duty, and has a squadron of sister ships somewhere nearby."

Signal lanterns were raised to the foremasthead, asking the *Cabot*, as the ship nearest the stranger, to engage the attention of the latter. But before the captain of the *Cabot* could comply it was seen that the distant ship had come about and was making straight for the two American vessels.

The decks of the *Alfred* and *Cabot* were immediately cleared for action. No drums were beat, or other unnecessary noise made. The men worked swiftly, went silently to their quarters; the batteries were masked and lights placed behind, while ammunition was hurried up from the magazine-room by the powder-monkeys, the youngest members of the crew.

The stranger bore down upon them. Presently came a hail from her deck: "Who are you, and whither are you bound?"

The *Cabot* made answer: "This is the *Betsy*, from Plymouth. Who are you?"

Every ear was strained to catch the answer. It came ringing over the clear water through the still night air:

"His Majesty's ship *Glasgow*, of twenty-four guns!"

As the *Alfred's* battery consisted of the same number of long 9-pounders on the gun deck and six 6-pounders on the quarter-deck it was apparent that, if the stranger had not lied, her strength in guns must be at least a match for the Britisher. In addition to this, the American flag-ship had the support of the little *Cabot*, with her own fourteen guns and crew of two hundred. Commodore Hopkins felt a great relief when he noted this. The American crews thought they would make short work of the enemy. But not so Paul Jones. He had already seen too much incompetence displayed on that cruise to feel anything but serious misgivings.

It was now two-thirty in the morning. The moon had gone down. Evidently in the darkness that prevailed the *Glasgow* was ignorant of the fact that there were other American ships in the little squadron, else she would have approached with greater caution. As it happened they did not come up during the fray which ensued, and took practically no part at all in it.

The *Cabot* had now got very close to the lee bow of the enemy, and suddenly poured a broadside into her. Instantly the British ship seemed to wake up to her danger. She wore around with all haste, and ran off to clear for action. In twenty minutes she bore down again, this time with a grimness of purpose that there was no mistaking.

Paul Jones was in command of the gun deck. The *Alfred* was so heavily laden with war trophies that she was down in the water almost to her portsills; but the sea was calm and her lowness in no wise prevented the free use of both her batteries, which were used with the utmost ferocity.

The fighting was kept up until daybreak. The *Glasgow* was hulled a number of times, her mainmast was deeply scarred, her sails and rigging well riddled with shot. But she had disabled the little *Cabot* at the second broadside from her big guns, and had then concentrated her attention on the *Alfred* with such good marksmanship that the wheelblock of the American was carried away and she came helplessly up into the wind in such a position that the enemy poured in several disastrous broadsides before her head could be regained. In this maneuver such poor seamanship was displayed on the part of Commodore Hopkins and Captain Saltonstall that Paul Jones fairly boiled within himself; but he could only hold his peace at the time. Later on, in letters to his friends, he gave full vent to his disgust at the way the American ships were handled; for only one commanding officer— Captain Biddle, of the *Andrew Doria*, who gave futile but heroic chase to the *Glasgow*—did he have particular praise.

When, with the coming of morning, the British ship retired, she was suffered to get away by Commodore Hopkins. He seemed to be glad that she had not stayed to do them worse damage. The brave American seamen fumed in the privacy of the fo'c'sl' on that voyage in. Old Bill Putters cursed at every breath whenever he was out of an officer's sight.

The Government held two courts-martial following the *Glasgow* affair. As a result Captain Hazard, of the *Providence*, was dishonorably dismissed from service, and numerous other officers censured, among them Commodore Hopkins. Undoubtedly the latter would have met with dismissal except for powerful political influences brought to bear in his behalf.

- 35 -

VIII

THE YOUNG CAPTAIN

Although there was a subtle estrangement between Commodore Hopkins and Paul Jones, each respected the other's character. At the close of the inglorious expedition which we have dealt with, the senior officer came to the conclusion that it would be far less embarrassing to both concerned were the first-lieutenant of the *Alfred* placed on some ship other than that occupied by the chief of the squadron himself.

Therefore, with more adroitness than he had displayed in meeting the enemy, Commodore Hopkins managed to induce Congress to offer the energetic Scotchman a berth as commander of the *Providence*, in the place of the dismissed Captain Hazard. He also permitted him to take with him a few of his favorite men, among this number Wannashego, the young Indian. The latter's joy knew no bounds at this turn of events. His stoical Indian nature prevented any marked display of his satisfaction, but his demeanor could not wholly hide it from the attention of his Scotch friend.

"Now," declared Wannashego, with shining eyes, "I sure we will see some heap big fighting. If I stay on that other ship, *Alfred*, one day longer I sure run away to the whaler-ship or my people. That *Alfred* no brave-ship; just squaw-ship—'fraid to fight!"

Paul Jones smiled in sympathy. He too had felt like a different man since the announcement of the change. Now that he had full and absolute control of an American ship himself, he determined he should show his countrymen and the enemy what he could really do.

The *Providence*, his new ship, was a small sloop of fourteen guns and about a hundred men. She was far from a pretentious vessel to look at, but Paul Jones's sharp eyes detected in her certain lines which augured for speed, and when he once got her out into the broad reaches of the Atlantic he found that in this surmise of her sailing abilities he had not been misled. For her size she was a remarkably good sailer.

For a time the *Providence* was kept employed in transporting men and supplies along the shores at the eastern entrance of Long Island Sound, and as this was done in the face of numerous British ships which hovered around like so many hornets, the reputation of the new commanding officer soon began to grow.

On August 21 Paul Jones sailed on a six-weeks' cruise—a cruise which historians have termed the first cruise of an American man-of-war. At least it was the first to be noted by an enemy—the first that shed any degree of glory on the flag of the new Republic, whose Declaration of Independence had been signed less than seven weeks previously.

It was a venture worthy of the Vikings and their rude boats, for the seas swarmed with English frigates outranking the little vessel in everything except the alertness of her commander and the courage of her crew. From Bermuda to the Banks of Newfoundland he boldly sailed, defying the fastest ships of the enemy to catch him, and striking terror to British merchantmen and fishermen.

During the first week of September the *Providence* sighted a large ship which she mistook for an Indiaman homeward bound. This stranger proved to be the *Solebay*, British frigate of twenty guns. Too late the *Providence* discovered her error; there was no chance to withdraw in dignity.

The *Solebay* immediately made for the American, who took to her heels, relying upon her good sailing qualities to escape, as she had on many another such occasion. But the Britisher proved she was no mean sailer herself. In fact, she began to overhaul her foe.

The day was warm and clear. A strong breeze was blowing from the northeast. The little *Providence* was legging it briskly over the wind-tossed waters. But the *Solebay* gained on her every hour.

The chase had started about noon. By four o'clock the frigate was almost within gunshot. The heart of everybody except the commander was in the lower regions of his jacket. Paul Jones was serene enough; his confidence seemed not one whit lessened. Presently he displayed the reason for his attitude.

"Look," said he to his chief officer, as he handed him a glass; "do you not notice that his broadside guns are still unleashed? He thinks he can take us by firing his bow-chaser. What foolishness! Nothing would be easier than for us to bear away before the wind and run under his broadside."

Nearly every ounce of canvas on the *Providence* had been flung to the breeze. Still the *Solebay* drew closer.

"He should know who we are before we leave him," declared Paul Jones, with a grim smile. He uttered a quick order. The next moment the American colors fluttered out at the masthead.

To their surprise the *Solebay* acknowledged the courtesy by also running up the American emblem.

"He cannot deceive us by that," said Paul Jones. "His lines tell me as plain as day he is British. But wait; I shall show him something in a moment!"

He called out to the man at the wheel: "Give her a good full, Quartermaster!"

"A good full, sir!" came back the instant acknowledgment.

Paul Jones then ordered the studding-sails set. The next moment the helm was put about, and before the astonished crew on the *Solebay* knew what was happening, the American sloop ran directly under his broadside, and went off dead before the wind.

The British frigate came about in haste and confusion. But by the time she was under headway again, the American ship was far off, her newly-trimmed studding-sails bellying to the breeze and gaining speed at every leap and bound. Needless to say, the *Solebay* was now out of the running, a very crestfallen enemy. Such clever maneuvering her commander had never witnessed before.

Three weeks later the *Providence* was saucily threading northern waters.

One day, off Cape Sable, Wannashego and several others of the sailors asked permission to try to catch some of the splendid fish which abounded in those cold waters. As they had been on salt provisions for a long while, Paul Jones readily consented, and the ship was hoved to. The men got out their lines, and soon began to haul in some fine specimens of the finny tribe.

While they fished, a sharp lookout was kept for danger from the British. It was well this was done, apparently, for presently a sail was made out to windward of them. At once the fishing stopped, the *Providence* set some of her light sails, and the anchor was hauled in.

As the stranger approached, Paul Jones convinced himself that she was no such sailer as the *Solebay*, and making sure a little later that she was a British warship he determined to amuse himself with her. He communicated his plans to his officers, and patiently waited for the frigate, which turned out to be His Majesty's ship, the *Milford*.

The young captain made no move until the British craft got almost within range, whereupon he doubled on her quarter and sped away under restrained speed on the new course. Mistaking the rate she was traveling at to be her best, and cheered at the thought of over-taking her, the English captain took up the chase with gusto. For seven or eight hours the pursuit continued, all this time the *Providence* cunningly keeping just beyond gunshot of her enemy, yet seeming to exert herself to the limit in maintaining her position.

Finally getting discouraged at his want of success, the Britisher began firing. Turning to his chief marine officer, Paul Jones said: "Direct one of your men to load his musket, and as often as yonder enemy salutes our flag with her great guns, do you have your man reply with his musket!"

A broad grin spread over the marine officer's face. He soon had his man stationed on the quarter-deck, and the next time the frigate rounded to and sent a futile broadside in the direction of the *Providence*, the marine elevated his musket and banged away. Several times this performance, a perfect burlesque in the quaintness of its humor, was indulged in. And each time, as the comparatively mild report of the musket followed the roar of the enemy's big guns, the American sailors laughed uproariously and cheered.

"We have had our fun now, my men," said Paul Jones. "This fellow has swallowed our bait gloriously; the time has come for us to stop *fishing* and go about our business."

He thereupon ordered more sail spread, and in a short time the astonished *Milford*—which he would have attempted to capture had she not clearly been a more powerful vessel—was left well behind. Although he did not know it then, the Scotch captain was to meet this foe again within the year.

Before he returned, this bold tiger of the sea succeeded in capturing sixteen British vessels. He also made an attack on Canso, Nova Scotia, thereby releasing several American prisoners; burned three vessels belonging to the Cape Breton fishery; and in a descent on the Isle of Madame destroyed several large fishing-smacks.

When at last Paul Jones reached his own shores again he left behind him a terrorized enemy who since that cruise have ever called him a buccaneer and pirate. Why England should regard this valiant sea-fighter, who never needlessly shed a drop of blood, or took a penny's-worth of spoils out of the larder of war, in this insulting light, its countrymen have never satisfactorily explained. But we do know that Lord Nelson himself was never a cleaner fighter; that the very brilliancy and extreme daring of Paul Jones's exploits stunned his enemy, and left them in a species of stupefaction.

Welcomed home with unusual acclaim, Paul Jones found that during his absence two things had happened which vitally concerned him. One thing was the ravaging of his plantation by the British. His fine buildings now lay in ashes, he was told. His splendid heifers had gone to satisfy the appetites of the raiding soldiers under Lord Dunmore. His slaves, who had become to him "a species of grownup children," had been carried off to die under the pestilential lash of cruel overseers in Jamaica canefields, while the price of their poor bodies swelled the pockets of English slave-dealers. To his great pleasure, however, he learned that his own overseer, canny old Duncan Macbean, had gotten away and joined General Morgan's riflemen, presumably there to wreak vengeance on the Red-coats with John Paul's own trusty rifle.

This was indeed a hard blow to the young captain who, in commenting upon it, wrote to Mr. Hewes: "It appears that I have no fortune left but my sword, and no prospect except that of getting alongside the enemy."

The second bit of news was the belated notification that, while he was away on his cruise, Congress, on October 10, 1776, had made him a commissioned captain in the United States Navy. It might be expected that such an announcement would be very gratifying to him, but not so. Paul Jones received it with more bitterness of spirit than pleasure, for he was only number eighteen in the list of appointees. This was an injustice which he never forgot, and to which the sensitive fellow referred all through his subsequent life. He thought he ought to have been not lower than sixth in rank, because, by the law of the previous year, there were only five captains ahead of him. In the meantime, too, he had done good service, while the new captains ranking above him were untried.

If Paul Jones had a failing it was that of desire for prestige. Rank was to him a passion, not merely because it would enable him to be more effective, but for its own sake. He liked all the signs of display—titles, epaulets, medals, busts, marks of honor of all kinds. "How near to the heart of every military or naval officer is rank, which opens the door to glory!" he wrote. But, mind you, Paul Jones did not have the "swelled head." He never once over-estimated his abilities, inwardly or outwardly; and he desired fame because he knew he was entitled to it. If the reward failed to come after he had qualified for and performed the service, he felt cheated—just as the day-laborer feels cheated when he does his task and is not paid his wage.

On November 4, 1776, Paul Jones was placed in command of the *Alfred*, the ship on which he had made his first cruise as a first-lieutenant some nine months earlier. In company with the *Providence*, now under the command of Captain Hacker, he made a cruise of about a month, captured seven merchant ships, several of which carried valuable supplies to the British army, and again cleverly avoided the superior enemy frigates. While making for port they encountered armed transports, the *Mellish* and the *Bideford*, both of which had been separated from their convoy, the *Milford*, in a terrific gale. Although larger and heavier ships in every way, the Americans attacked and captured them. Shortly afterward the *Milford*, accompanied by a British letter-of-marque, put in an appearance, and gave chase. Once more Paul Jones was too clever for the British frigate. He outsailed and outmaneuvered her, getting away with all his prizes except the smaller of the transports, which had fallen astern.

After his return, in early December, from the cruise in the *Alfred*, Paul Jones served on the Board of Advice to the Marine Committee, and was very useful in many ways. He urged strongly the necessity of making a cruise in European waters for the sake of moral persuasion, and offered to lead such an expedition. His energy and dashing character made a strong impression on Lafayette, who was then in the country, and who heartily supported the project. He wrote a letter to General Washington, strongly recommending that Paul Jones be made head of such an expedition.

About the same time the young captain had an interview with Washington, in which he appealed against what he considered another injustice. The *Trumbull*—one of the fine new American frigates just completed and built in New Amsterdam in accordance with Paul Jones's own plans—had been placed under the command of Captain Saltonstall, whom the Scotchman considered incompetent.

Paul Jones did not get the *Trumbull* after all; but the interview was not without its effect. A little later the Marine Committee ordered him to enlist seamen for his suggested European cruise. And on June 14, 1777, Congress appointed him to the command of the sloop-of-war *Ranger*, of eighteen guns.

IX

ABOARD THE "RANGER"

When Paul Jones was ordered to Portsmouth to command the new sloop-of-war *Ranger*, Congress allowed him to take with him a few of his favorite petty officers. Of course among this number was Wannashego, the young Narragansett. The bold Scotch captain had formed a strong liking for Wannashego, whom he had found not only an able boatswain's mate and an impetuous fighter, but one most devoted to his own interests. Indeed, the young Indian fairly worshiped the decking his splendid officer trod. They had served together ever since their first meeting, going from the *Alfred* to the *Providence*, then back to the *Alfred* again. And now they were once more to be together—this time in a long and probably stirring voyage across the big sea, right into the very home-waters of the enemy himself! No wonder the heart of Wannashego stirred with happy expectation.

Another old shipmate to accompany Paul Jones on the new expedition, but one hitherto unmentioned, was Nathaniel Fanning, now a third-lieutenant. From this friend, a very keen observer of our hero at all times, as well as a man of more than ordinary intelligence, we get the following interesting description of Paul Jones:

"He was about middle height, so slender as to be wiry, so lithe as to be compared to a panther, so quick in his movements that we sailors often spoke of him as 'swifter than chain-lightning.' His face was as brown as an Indian's. His eyes under ordinary conditions were a steel-gray; but in moments of excitement you would swear they were as black as coal and emitting sparks. Though he was not at all big, his neck, arms, and shoulders were those of a heavy-set man, with a chest that did you good to see. The strength of his arms and shoulders could hardly be believed; and he had equal use of both hands, even to writing with the left as well as with the right. He was a past-master in the art of boxing; though there were many hard nuts to crack in the various crews he commanded, I never knew him to come out second best. When aroused, he could strike blows and do more damage in a second than any man I ever saw could do in a minute. He always fought as if that was what he was made for; it was only when he was perfectly at peace that he seemed uneasy and restless.

"He was never petulant toward those under him. Even in cases of failure to carry out his orders, or meet his expectations, he would be lenient. But if he detected you in any act that was wilful or malicious, he would assail you like a tiger. He was not a quarrelsome man; but he was the easiest person in the world for a quarrelsome man to pick a quarrel with. Good men all liked him; sneaks and tyrants hated him bitterly."

We may add that all records go to show that Paul Jones was as much a father to his crew as he was a commander. He interested the sailors in the smallest details of their work, gave them lessons in rope-splicing, or reproved a young chap for his "lubberly walk" with a personal demonstration of the correct swagger to be kept in mind by Jack afloat. At the same time, with all this kindness of heart, he did not let a single man take advantage of his goodness. "I tell you, my men," he said on one occasion, "when I become convinced that a sailor of mine must be given the 'cat' I will not leave it to be done by the uncertain arm of others; but I will do it *myself*—and so confounded quick that it will make your heads swim!"

On the very same day—June 14, 1777—that Paul Jones was appointed commander of the *Ranger*, Congress selected the permanent flag of the United States—the good old Stars-and-Stripes which we still have. Up to this time nobody had really been satisfied with the "Rattlesnake" emblem; Paul Jones particularly objected to it. Now Mrs. Betsey Ross, of Philadelphia, was busy at work making the first new flag from a rough pencil sketch furnished her by General Washington.

When Paul Jones heard of the adoption of the new emblem, and saw plans for it, he was greatly pleased. He took out his own pencil, quickly copied the plans, and stuck the paper in his pocket.

As soon as possible he proceeded to Portsmouth, and immediately entered upon the task of outfitting the *Ranger* for sea. He found the ship to be a fine-looking craft, built expressly for speed, with a length six feet greater than the regular 20-gun vessel of the day. But he thought her spars too heavy, and ordered his shipwright to "fid them about four feet lower in the hounds," which was done. He also had fourteen long 9-pounders and four 6-pounders put in place of the regular twenty 6-pound guns intended, and made other changes looking toward her seaworthiness. He was very proud of her coppered hull, shining like burnished gold—the first hull thus covered in the new country.

As the work of outfitting went on, he had the goodwill and interest of the entire colonial town. Busy though he was he did not neglect the social side of life here any more than he had elsewhere when on land; for Paul Jones loved elegance and display, intercourse with the fair sex; and his splendid bearing, immaculate dress, magnetic personality, keen wit—to say nothing of his record of daring deeds—made him extremely popular in all gatherings, particularly where hoop-skirts abounded. Many a good dame in

America did her utmost to marry the gallant young captain off to her own daughter or another admiring damsel. But it was no use; Paul Jones, while always professing the greatest respect and kindliest interest in his feminine associates, never allowed them to turn his well-balanced head.

Thus in his social activities there in Portsmouth, the captain of the *Ranger* escorted bevies of charming and vivacious damsels and their mamas and papas aboard the ship and explained her many wonders, and discoursed on what she probably would do to the English. Then one day he whispered mysteriously to some of them, and forthwith these pretty Colonial girls spoke to others. The consequence was, that soon afterward there was a merry gathering at the home of one of the maids. A "quilting bee" they termed it; but there, fashioned amid chat and laughter, amid sober thought and spirit of service to country, slender fingers cut and sewed together the silken portions of a beautiful American flag—the first one of stars and stripes that anybody in that locality had yet seen. From time to time these fair workers looked for guidance to a pencilled sketch furnished them by their chosen knight. Treasured wedding and court dresses of some of their mothers furnished rare patches of blue, and lengths of red and white, and these grew into beautiful five-pointed stars and graceful stripes under the girls' careful handiwork.

During this time Paul Jones was putting the finishing touches to the *Ranger* and impatiently awaiting the dispatches he was to carry from his Government to the American Commission in France. At midnight of the 31st of October these official documents were delivered to him by a courier who had covered one hundred and forty miles, eating and sleeping in his saddle. Among the papers was the news of the surrender of Burgoyne.

Nothing now prevented Paul Jones from making sail on his long cruise. The *Ranger* was in readiness, the wind good. But before making sail there was one ceremony he must not forget.

The new flag—his gift from the patriotic Portsmouth girls—must be unfurled to the breeze. And they must see it! By horse he sent Wannashego galloping to the homes of each of the five young seamstresses. In an hour they appeared, eager and excited, despite the fact that most of the good people of the town were fast asleep.

With simple ceremony but eloquent suggestion the splendid banner, under the impulse of Paul Jones's own hands, went up to the *Ranger's* peak. As it spread out to the breeze under the star-lit sky, the Scotch captain said, with a deep feeling none could help noticing: "That flag and I are twins. Born the same hour from the same womb of destiny, we cannot be parted in life or in death. So long as we can float we shall float together. If we must sink, we shall go down as one!"

To the courier who had brought the dispatches, Paul Jones now turned. He handed him the receipt for the papers, and on its back he wrote: "I shall spread this news in France within thirty days."

When the shore people had taken their departure, cheered by the crew of the *Ranger* and leaving their own good wishes behind, Captain Jones immediately got under way. He took a northerly course, thereby hoping to avoid most of the enemy's cruisers, so that his dispatches could be delivered as soon as possible.

He left no record except the *Ranger's* log; but Mr. Hall, who was the ship's carpenter, gives some details of the trip which are far from uninteresting:

"I had sailed with many captains in all sorts of voyages, but I had never seen a ship crowded the way Captain Jones crowded the *Ranger*. He held to his northerly route, though the wind was adverse, hanging all the time between north-northeast and east-northeast. It veered slightly at times, but you could count on it being forward of the beam on a true course, and often it was near dead ahead. Imagine, then, the situation of the ship's crew, with a top-heavy and cranky craft under their feet, and a commander who day and night insisted on every rag she could stagger under without laying clear down!

"As it was, she came close to beam ends more than once, and on one occasion she righted only by us letting the fly-sheets go with hatchets. During all this trying time Captain Jones was his own navigating officer, keeping the deck eighteen or twenty hours out of every twenty-four, often serving extra grog to the drenched men with his own hands, and by his example silencing all disposition to grumble. In the worst of it the watch was lap-watched. This brought the men eight hours on and four off. There was no better way to arrange it; but for all that a good many of them began to growl. These fellows had all been shipped from Portsmouth, induced to enlist by unwise glowing accounts of the Government of the rich prize-money that would probably be made on the trip. Now, when they found the captain avoiding the enemy rather than seeking him out, and were subjected to such a terrific bit of sailing, they became dissatisfied.

"At first Captain Jones was mighty angry, but as soon as he satisfied himself that the Government had really been in error, he acted splendidly by the men. He told them that he would personally guarantee them a fair revenue from prizes later on; more than that, from his own pocket he advanced them 147 guineas, to make up the difference in wages thus far allowed them by Congress but which the Marine Committee had been unable to make good on account of the poverty of the States. They quieted down then, apparently satisfied, cheering their commander well. But Lieutenant Simpson, who had really instigated the mutiny, did not escape so easily.

Wannashego, an Indian boatswain's mate, had caught Simpson stirring the men up to trouble, reported it to Captain Jones, and the latter had the officer put in irons for the rest of the voyage."

As Mr. Hall says in this account, the weather was bad and the voyage tempestuous. But nevertheless there were times when the tired men sought recreation in story and song, as seamen always will do, and often over the dashing waters the following refrain, composed by Midshipman Charley Bell, went echoing:

"So now we had him hard and fast,Burgoyne laid down his arms at last,And that is why we brave the blastTo carry the news to London!Heigh-ho! car-r-y the news;Go carry the news to London!Yes car-r-y, car-r-y,Carry the news to London!"

During the last two days' run the *Ranger* took two merchantmen loaded with wines and dried fruit and bound for London. Paul Jones put prize-crews aboard, sending one on to Brest and keeping the other with him. West of Ushant they spoke a Dutch East Indiaman, whereupon the Scotch captain informed the Dutch commander of the surrender of Burgoyne and dryly asked him to "kindly repeat the news, with my compliments, to any British captain met."

A little later, on the 2d of December, the saucy *Ranger* and her prize dropped anchor in the Loire, below Nantes, France.

X

IN THE ENEMY'S OWN WATERS

One of the first things which Paul Jones did on landing on French soil was to seek out Dr. Benjamin Franklin, who, with Silas Deane and Arthur Lee, were his country's foreign commissioners. He found these diplomats domiciled in the fine home of Monsieur De Chaumont, a wealthy Frenchman with strong sympathies for the Colonists.

It was the first meeting of Paul Jones and Benjamin Franklin—a meeting marked with much gratification on the part of each. It was also the beginning of a personal friendship long-lasting and very helpful to the Scotch adventurer. Before its conclusion the caller learned, with some chagrin, that he was not the first to bring news across the sea of the surrender of General Burgoyne; that Mr. John Austen, of Boston, had sailed in a French merchantman a day or two earlier, and by reason of the shorter course, had arrived somewhat ahead of him. However, Austen's news was mere hearsay, lacking the details and authenticity of Captain Jones's dispatches.

It had been the intention of the American commissioners to give Paul Jones the *Indien*—a fine frigate building secretly at Amsterdam—on his arrival. But this proved to be one more of his disappointments, for the British minister to the Netherlands had recently discovered the destination of the vessel, and had made such protests of a breach of neutrality that the commissioners had been forced to sell the ship to France.

To his previous acquaintance with the Duc and Duchesse De Chartres there is no doubt that Paul Jones owed his introduction at this time into French society. The Duchesse herself had been, before her marriage, the richest heiress in France. While her husband was a spendthrift, and a man of lax morals generally, she was highly respected in all communities. This noble family lived in a charming chateau, with even more charming gardens, on the outskirts of Paris, and as soon as they heard of the arrival of the already famous Scotch captain they sent him an urgent invitation to call.

This he did. An enjoyable meeting resulted, and he was royally entertained. Later, at a ball given in his honor and attended by the élite of the social world, he met a beautiful young lady named Aimée de Telusson, the adopted daughter of King Louis XV. Mademoiselle De Telusson, after the king died, had been supported by a pension from the monarch's court, and had lived with her protectoress, Madame De Marsan, under the patronage of several great ladies, of whom the Duchesse De Chartres was one.

Paul Jones was greatly fascinated with the fair Aimée, a feeling which she seemed to reciprocate. As they became better and better acquainted she fairly idolized him, and on his part he thought her the most perfect specimen of womanhood he had ever seen. Although he must have known that she was very much in love with him, this gallant seaman who was admired by all the people of France, never declared his own love to her.

Dr. Franklin wished to keep Paul Jones in European waters, there to harass the British shipping. On the other hand Lee, who for some reason entertained a jealousy and dislike for the Scotchman, was bent on getting him back in American waters as soon as he could. Silas Deane, the third commissioner, was a nonentity, with little voice in the matter. However, Dr. Franklin had his way; he thundered forth his orders that Paul Jones was to stay on that side of the sea—and Paul Jones stayed. To say that he was grateful to the stout-hearted, venerable statesman is saying no more than the truth.

After some delay Dr. Franklin advised him that arrangements had been completed by the commission for him to convoy a number of American merchant vessels from Nantes into Quiberon Bay, where a large French fleet, under Admiral La Motte Picquet, lay waiting with the intention of sailing for America. Such protection by French warships a week earlier would have been a distinct breach of neutrality, but now the much-talked-of "Treaty of Alliance" had been made between France and America, and henceforth France could not only openly sympathize with the new Republic but could take up arms in her behalf.

Of course Paul Jones was glad at this turn of events. He was pleased for his country's sake; pleased for his own sake, because the situation promised easier working out of his plans.

But it seemed that his troubles were not yet entirely over. When he reached the anchorage of the *Ranger* he found the crew in a sad disruption. It appeared that the profligate Simpson, who had been freed from his irons upon the ship reaching port, had been working the men into a mutiny by declaring he had heard that their captain had left them in the lurch. Except for the confidence expressed in Paul Jones by the majority of his officers and some of the sailors, among whom of course was Wannashego, it is doubtful if the commander would have found very many of his crew left upon his arrival. As it stood, the malcontents were still arguing with the loyal when he put in an appearance.

Upon learning the cause of the trouble his Scotch ire was so thoroughly aroused against Simpson that it is hard to guess what he would have done to him, had the miscreant not made a plausible excuse for securing what he termed his "misinformation" and uttered voluble apologies for his part in the affair.

As soon as order could be obtained, the commander began to refit for the new enterprise. The craft's masts were re-shortened and other defects of structure remedied in an effort to put her on a better keel. Then in company with a tender, the brig *Independence*, the American sloop-of-war set sail. A little later, flying the Stars-and-Stripes at her masthead, she anchored off the bay at Quiberon.

Without delay Paul Jones sent a small boat off to the French admiral, desiring to know, if he saluted the admiral's ship, whether her commander would return the salute.

When the reply came back it was in the affirmative. Thereupon Paul Jones brought the *Ranger* into the bay. She hove to, and the next moment her guns thundered thirteen times. Promptly the courtesy was returned by nine guns from the admiral's ship, it being the French custom to fire four guns less than a saluting Republic. It was too dark to bring in the *Independence* for her share in the proceeding, but the next morning this little vessel sailed proudly between two parallel lines of the fine French fleet, flying her American flag, and in answer to her own guns there was returned another recognition of America as a nation.

Returning to Nantes, Paul Jones sent Dr. Franklin a joyous letter, telling him about the honor paid the American flag for the first time by another country.

The *Ranger* was held in port following this until April 10, 1778. In the interval her commander had the good fortune to be much in the company of the Duc and Duchesse De Chartres and the charming Mademoiselle Aimée De Telusson. The day previous to the date of sailing of his vessel, the Duchesse paid him the compliment of giving a dinner in his honor. At this many distinguished families were present, as well as prominent army and navy officers. During the course of festivities, the Madame graciously presented her popular guest with a richly-jewelled watch which she said had belonged to her grandfather, Louis XIV.

Paul Jones bowed, and replied with fine gallantry: "May it please your Royal Highness, if fortune should favor me at sea I will some day lay an English frigate at your dainty feet!"

The next morning the *Ranger* put out to sea again. With the salt spray dashing in his nostrils, with every fiber of his adventure-loving soul thrilling once more in expectation of a brush with the enemy, Paul Jones forgot the tameness of politics and the foibles of social functions.

With gusto he took a brigantine in the Irish Sea on the 14th, and sank her. Then proceeding into St. George's Channel he ran onto the *Lord Chatham*, a British merchant ship bound from London to Dublin. This vessel was valuable enough to keep as a prize, so the Scotch captain manned her with a prize crew and had them take her to Brest.

Paul Jones now headed farther northward along the coast of England. In his mind he was formulating an exceedingly daring plan, none less than a sudden descent upon Whitehaven, the seaport he knew so well as a boy and from which he had made his first voyage to America. If he could dash into Whitehaven, destroy most of the immense shipping which was always harbored there, and thereby effect an exchange of prisoners in Europe, he thought the risk would well be worth while.

But when he arrived in the vicinity of his old headquarters, the winds were so contrary to his purpose that he gave up the project for the time being. For the next few days he cruised along the southern coast of Scotland on the lookout for other enemy prizes. Nothing of great moment occurred, and with better weather conditions than had previously prevailed, he made up his mind again to try an attack on Whitehaven.

The hills were covered with snow when the *Ranger* came within sight of them. In the harbor of the town of some fifty thousand inhabitants were collected almost three hundred merchant-ships and fishing-smacks. The captain had carefully let down the portlids to conceal his guns, and adopted whatever other means he could devise for concealing the nature of his ship.

Paul Jones determined to wait for night to perform his operations. He would need the screen of darkness. When that hour had come he ordered every man mustered on deck. Then he announced his plan to them and finished by saying tersely: "I call for thirty volunteers to assist me in this task of reprisal for the numerous burnings the British have put upon us in America. No man need engage in this enterprise unless he wishes to. But those who share with me its dangers shall also share with me its glories."

It seemed as if every man on deck shouted, "Aye, sir!" As might be expected Wannashego, the young Narragansett, was among the first.

Paul Jones smiled with satisfaction. "With so many volunteers I see I shall have to choose my thirty men from among you. The strongest and most active are the ones I want."

He then proceeded to make his selections. When he was done he noticed that he had forgotten the faithful Indian youth. "I shall make it thirty-one, on second thought," he said promptly, and at once called upon the happy Wannashego to step forth with the other volunteers.

It was a little after midnight when, with his men in two boats, Paul Jones left the *Ranger*. It was so far in to the piers that it was almost dawn when they finally arrived at one of the outer ones. All haste must be made or the light of the approaching day would disclose their movements and prevent their success.

Paul Jones ordered one boat, under the direction of Mr. Hill and Lieutenant Wallingford, to proceed on the north side of the harbor and set fire to the shipping there, while with the second party the commander went to the other side, to perform a similar work.

Two grim-looking forts rose up in the darkness, one facing each section of harbor. In order to render the guns in these harmless, Paul Jones and Wannashego were now set ashore, and while they began stealthily and swiftly to approach the first forts, their crew started off to set fire to the shipping on the south.

The Scotch captain and young Indian had a very delicate task facing them. Before they could spike the cannon the sentinels must be secured. Stealing along in the shadows of the great walls of the first fort, they discovered that all of the guardsmen were unsuspiciously enjoying a game of cards in the guard-house itself. As quick as lightning Paul Jones and Wannashego sprang forward and barred the door, making the men prisoners. Then, without loss of time, the two Americans began scaling the walls of the fort. When the cannon here had been successfully spiked, they hurried to the second fort, a quarter of a mile distant, and in the same manner confined the sentinels there and spiked the guns.

This was surely a daring exploit for two to perform, when the alarm might be sounded any moment and the whole town swoop down upon them.

After the task had been performed, Paul Jones naturally expected to see the fires which his parties were to start. To his great disappointment no welcome flare showed itself in either direction. In the dim light of early dawn—that alarming dawn, so little desired—the captain hurried forward, only to discover that the party under Mr. Hill and Mr. Wallingford were in considerable confusion. The fires they had ignited had refused to burn, and their candles had gone out as well. It was the same situation with the other party; their candles also had gone out, and there seemed no way to relight them.

Although the day was coming on apace and danger of discovery grew with it, the dauntless Scotch commander would not give up his project until every expedient had been exhausted. Placing sentinels to guard against a surprise, he sent Wannashego and a few men to the nearest house. The inmates were forced to deliver lights for the candles. With the aid of these a fire was soon started in the steerage of a large ship, which was in the midst of a hundred or more others. To make sure that this blaze would not burn out, a barrel of tar was placed upon it. In a short time flames were springing up out of all hatchways in the vessel.

Now the inhabitants of the town began to appear in hundreds. Individuals ran angrily toward the burning ship, bent on extinguishing the flames before they should communicate to the adjoining vessels.

"They must not be permitted to put out this fire now or our plans are ruined completely!" cried Paul Jones. With the words he sprang between the ship and the foremost of those running up, drew two pistols from his belt, and leveled them at the angry faces.

"One step nearer and some of you will be dead men!" cried the Scotch captain. "Back with you as fast as you came, else by the eternal day and night you shall feel this lead!"

"Why, it's Paul Jones!" called somebody in the throng, who recognized him.

Instantly the crowd fell back in fright. Not a man among them but who had heard of the things this daredevil had already done to the ships of their countrymen.

Paul Jones smiled grimly, as the people continued to retreat before his menacing pistols. Nor did he once leave his post until the ship back of him was a mass of flames and the whole shipping in the neighborhood hopelessly afire from it. Then he stepped coolly down into one of his boats, which had been brought up, and in company with the other, without the loss of a single man, he went back to the *Ranger*.

If the attempt had been made an hour earlier it is impossible to estimate the damage the Americans might have done, but dawn saved the town of Whitehaven, also half of the shipping. Paul Jones was disappointed because his plans had in a measure miscarried. But he had accomplished much for his country just the same. The excitement along the coast was intense. Every English port, nervous and trembling, was on the watch for the bold invader. No Englishman felt safe so long as Paul Jones roamed the sea at will. Much less did British captains feel secure.

XI

OUTWITTING THE "DRAKE"

As the *Ranger* once more spread her sails and stood out to sea, Paul Jones turned to his first-lieutenant and said:

"Mr. Wallingford, have her head pointed across the Firth. There lays my old home-town of Arbigland which I have seen but once since I was twelve years old——"

"Pardon me, sir," interrupted the first officer; "surely you do not think of attacking your own birthplace?"

"Indeed not," was the sharp and somewhat impatient rejoinder. "Though it belongs to the enemy, that would be the act of a man without heart and conscience. Please hear me out. Not far from my home there lives in the same county of Kirkcudbright a most important personage to British interests. This is the Earl of Selkirk. In lieu of the only partial success of our descent upon Whitehaven I propose to even up matters this very day by calling upon the good earl and taking him hostage."

This was a daring conception, and Lieutenant Wallingford gasped. The *Ranger* was held to her new course, straight north across the Firth of Solway. When the ship came in view of the northern coast, her commander stood watching the high cliffs about Arbigland with a strange mixture of feelings. We shall never know exactly what thoughts stirred him, as he was a man not given to referring to his deeper sensations, but we may well infer that, in the short space of time he stood there studying the familiar landmarks of his care-free and happy boyhood, he lived over again the days of that period, climbed again the crags after sea-birds' eggs, sailed again his toy boats in the quiet coves.

St. Mary's Isle, a beautifully wooded promontory in the river Dee, was where the Earl of Selkirk lived in luxurious but quiet style. This was about a mile up the coast from Arbigland, and although Paul Jones had never met the Scotch nobleman or any of his family, he knew the location of the Selkirk broad acres as well as he knew the best fishing grounds in the Firth.

He landed on St. Mary's Isle with one boat and twelve men. Pointing out the path to take, and warning his men to commit no violence other than that which might be required in securing the earl himself, the captain awaited their return. In a short time they were back again, bringing a considerable quantity of silver plate, but without the earl, who they declared was not at home.

Paul Jones was very angry because his sailors had taken the silver plate. He used every argument except force in trying to get them to return it at once. When he saw that they were bent upon keeping the spoil, he said no more, but departed with them, for he knew well that the rules of war made confiscation perfectly legal.

Later on he wrote the Countess of Selkirk a long letter of apology and explanation, stating that he would exert every endeavor to return the plate to her. This he did, and succeeded, although in so doing it was necessary for him to go down into his own pocket for £150 in order to buy it back.

Paul Jones next turned his attention to an effort to capture the British man-of-war *Drake*, a vessel of twenty guns—two guns stronger than his own ship. This, too, was a bold undertaking, particularly in view of the fact that the *Drake* was known to carry a larger crew and was in her own waters. But the intrepid sea-king was not to be deterred. He had encountered this same vessel once before, several days before the attack on Whitehaven, when he was standing off Carrickfergus, and when she was anchored in the bay. During the night he had run in and tried to work into a position where he could board her quickly, surprise her crew, and overwhelm them before they could offer serious enough resistance to get aid from the big gray fortification which frowned down over the harbor from the massive heights above. But, owing to the strong wind which had prevailed at the time, the plan was frustrated; and the *Ranger* had quietly withdrawn to sea again without her foe knowing what a narrow escape she had met with.

Then Paul Jones had assuaged the disappointment of himself and his men with the remark: "Never mind, my brave fellows; that British sloop shall be ours yet, mark my words. When we are through with Whitehaven we shall look her up again."

And now the doughty captain meant to fulfil his promise!

On the morning of the 24th of April the *Ranger* was once more off Carrickfergus. The bay, the castled crag, the picturesque town, and the handsome British sloop-of-war, all stood out brilliantly in the clear sunlight.

But this time the American vessel was not destined to get in close to her enemy without suspicion. The very night before, word had been brought of the attack on Whitehaven, and as a consequence the entire populace of Carrickfergus was ready to look askance at the coming of every strange ship. As the *Ranger* appeared in the offing, therefore, she was immediately observed by the British aboard the *Drake*, and the American sailors could hear the creaking of the foe-ship's capstan and the hoarse rattle of the chains as her anchor was tripped in readiness for an emergency.

The *Ranger* now went completely about, her stern toward the shore. This was the best way possible to hide her identity, for it was seen that a boat was putting off from the English sloop and pulling toward them, apparently bent upon investigation. When the boat had approached within hailing distance of the American, one of its inmates—a British officer—stood up and cried: "What ship is that?"

Paul Jones, standing at his sailing-master's elbow, quietly prompted him in his answers.

"The *Saltandpepperforbritish*" replied Mr. Stacy so rapidly that all the words were a meaningless jumble to the Englishmen, who, however, caught the word "British" with some feeling of ease. Drawing a little closer, the officer repeated his question: "What ship is that? We cannot make out your answer."

"We've had fair winds, but glad to get in here," answered Mr. Stacy, pretending to have misunderstood the question.

There was an impatient remark from the British officer at this. He said something to his men. The boat of the enemy then drew up considerably nearer. By this time the craft was directly under the *Ranger's* quarter.

"I ask you for the third and last time, what ship is that?" hailed the British officer.

"And I answer again and for the last time, she is the *Lord Dunmore*, bound from Plymouth to London," called Mr. Stacy in an apparently exasperated voice. Then, again prompted by his captain, he went on: "Have you heard anything of that American cruiser which has been prowling about capturing merchant ships and frightening our coast people half out of their wits?"

"Yes," was the reply of the officer, now completely off his guard. "We would give a thousand pounds to meet her."

"If you will come aboard, our captain says he will give you further particulars about this impudent American," continued Mr. Stacy. "We think this news will aid you in finding him."

Unsuspiciously the British boat now came up, and a ladder was lowered over the port side. Just then one of the *Ranger's* own boats was dropped from the davits; it was quickly filled with men, and as the British officer clambered on deck and faced Paul Jones the American sailors made prisoners of his crew.

"What is the meaning of this?" cried the British officer. "Who are you, sir?"

"Captain Paul Jones," came the quick answer. "This is the American sloop-of-war *Ranger*, about which we promised you information. If you require further details, it is only proper for me to state that you are a prisoner of war on that ship at this moment!"

The officer uttered an exclamation of anger. But his chagrin was not greater than that of the other men aboard the boat when they were brought aboard and all sent below.

This whole proceeding had been witnessed from the *Drake* in a more or less hazy manner, but yet in a way to give the British aboard that vessel a fair idea of the catastrophe which had attended the efforts of their compatriots to learn the identity of the stranger. She immediately sent out alarm signals, and in a few minutes smoking bonfires along the entire headlands were relaying the startling intelligence to inland points.

In a little while the *Drake*, accompanied by five small vessels filled with townspeople curious to witness what they thought would be a battle, began to work out. She came very slowly, owing to an unfavorable tide. It was plain to be seen that her "dander was up;" that she meant to look into the plight of her boat's crew without further delay.

The *Ranger* now threw off every effort at disguise. Her portlids were run up, her guns run out, and everything put in trim for a hard fight. As the enemy came nearer and weathered the point, the *Ranger* cunningly and almost imperceptibly worked herself farther out into the channel where she would have more sea room for the engagement and be farther away from the guns of the fort. Thus led on, the *Drake* followed, slowly narrowing up the space between.

Now the British ship ran up her colors. At the same instant up went the Stars-and-Stripes aboard the American. Having come within hailing distance, the British commander, Captain Burden, called out: "Who are you?"

"The Continental ship *Ranger*," cried back Mr. Stacy, at word from Paul Jones. "Come on, we are waiting for you!"

Scarcely were the words spoken when the *Ranger's* helm was ported, and bringing her broadside to bear on the advancing ship, she roared out the first volley. The enemy at once returned the compliment. While her fire was spirited, somehow it lacked effectiveness, which is probably attributable to the distress and confusion caused on board of her by the stunning effect of the American's shooting. In a letter to Joseph Hewes, Paul Jones thus refers to the manner in which his men handled themselves: "We have seen that our men fight with courage on our own coasts. But no one has ever seen them fight on our coast as they fought here, almost in hail of the enemy's shore. Every shot told, and they gave the *Drake* three broadsides for two right along...."

On board the *Ranger*, Paul Jones walked the quarter-deck unharmed, amid a constant shower of musketry and the shriek of cannon-ball. Captain Burden, of the *Drake*, showed an equal disregard for danger, but within thirty minutes after the beginning of the fight he was mortally wounded by a musket shot in the head. Paul Jones was unaware of this fact until, during the hottest of the firing, his friend Wannashego glided quickly up to where he stood and announced the news.

"I am sorry for him, for he has shown himself to be a brave man; but it is the way of war," said the commander. "Did you see him shot, Wannashego?"

In his dusky hands the Indian youth held a musket whose barrel was hot to the touch and from which a tiny thread of smoke still curled. "I sure see British captain fall," he said with flashing eyes, as he patted his gun. "I take good aim at him. It is the first chance for me. Bang! They pick him up and carry him away."

With the words Wannashego hurried off, reloading his weapon as he ran. Paul Jones was thunderstruck. After a moment he muttered, "Poor Burden, your very importance in this conflict has caught the eagle eye of that young redskin and spelled your doom!"

The fighting continued fiercely. Twice was the ensign of the *Drake* shot away, and twice the gallant British tars rehoisted it. The enemy's fore and main topsail yards were completely riddled, the main topgallant mast and mizzen gaff hung up and down the spar, her jib dragged over her lee into the water, and her mainsails were a sieve of holes.

Never had Paul Jones seen men fight more tigerishly or with better aim than his were now doing. As the two ships were going off the wind, which was light, they both rolled considerably and together; in other words, when the *Ranger* went down to port the *Drake* came up to starboard. Quite early in the action, the Scotch captain had noticed that his quarter-gunners had caught the *Drake's* period of roll and were timing to fire as their muzzles went down and the enemy's came up. By this practice they were hulling the British ship prodigiously below her water-line and everywhere below her rail.

"What are you firing in that fashion for?" demanded Paul Jones of Midshipman Starbuck.

"To sink the British galoots, sir!"

"That is not my object," said the captain sharply. "Cease this destruction of the ship, and conduct yourselves so as to capture her instead."

The alert fellows instantly changed their tactics, and soon had the *Drake* an unmanageable log on the water, with her crew crying for quarter. When, after the desperate fighting of a little more than an hour, an accounting was taken it was found that the *Ranger* had suffered very little from the inaccurate fire of the British. True, she had lost two lives, among these Lieutenant Wallingford, and had six wounded; but her opponent had lost her commander and nineteen others killed, with twenty-eight officers and men wounded. The only officer remaining to strike her flag had been her second-lieutenant.

With a towline fastened to her prize, the *Ranger* now passed out of the lough and up St. George's Channel. About midnight she hove to, and there under the starlight the dead heroes of the conflict were sewn up in canvas and consigned to the deep with a fitting burial service.

With a valuable prize and more than one hundred and forty prisoners of war to look after, Paul Jones was now forced to give up his intention of cruising around Scotland. After taking a vessel off Malin Head he became further handicapped, and determined to make for Brest without additional delay.

And now came that long-dreamed-of and hoped-for hour when he was to enter a French port bringing a ship superior to his own—one belonging to the finest navy afloat, a feat which had never before happened in the history of naval warfare. As he sailed through the outer roads of Brest he was met by an escort of French warships, whose crews cheered lustily when they learned the identity of his prize.

It was past midnight when the *Ranger* let go anchor. Everything then seemed quiet, but like wildfire the news of the daring captain's return spread over the town. When daylight broke the quays were swarming with people, and the harbor was dotted with boats bearing passengers, all of whom were eager to catch a glimpse of the vanquished *Drake* and her conqueror.

XII

THE QUEER CONDUCT OF CAPTAIN LANDAIS

The next morning Captain Paul Jones woke up to find himself famous—almost overwhelmed with the praise and attentions of the naval officers of Brest as well as of all France. The Duc De Chartres was the first to come aboard, brimming with congratulations, and for the two days the *Ranger* lay in the harbor her decks thronged with officers of the French fleet and citizens who were eager to rejoice with the conqueror.

Then the other side of the picture began to show; the stern realities of France's disturbed political condition had to be faced. The *Ranger*, with her splendid prize, had gone to the deckyard for repairs, and the problem of feeding and clothing the three hundred men constituting his own crew and that of the *Drake* had to be met by Paul Jones. The Congress still owed him £1500 which he had advanced out of his own pocket for paying the crews of his former ships, the *Providence* and the *Alfred*, and this outlay had depleted his funds to such an extent that he had very little money left, so little that he now saw he would have to draw upon the commissioners a draft for 24,000 livres, which Congress had given him. To his annoyance the three commissioners promptly dishonored his draft. As a result, the merchant with whom he had contracted to refit the *Ranger* and the *Drake*, as well as to supply his crew and prisoners with provisions, declined to extend further credit.

This state of affairs put our hero in a very embarrassing position, and nettled him intensely. Had it not been for the fine friendship of such Frenchmen as the Duc De Chartres, Comte D'Orvillers, and M. Chaumont, through whose benevolence he was for a time able to feed and clothe his people, heal his wounded, and continue the refitting of his vessels, it is hard to tell what he would have done.

In the crude, undisciplined condition of the United States Navy in that day the crews could not seem to comprehend the idea that it was necessary to obey every order of the commander of a ship without raising a question. Almost at the instant of the engagement between the *Ranger* and the *Drake*, Lieutenant Simpson, the trouble-maker of the past, had used his influence in stirring up some of the crew to a state bordering on insubordination, telling them that being Americans fighting for liberty they had a right to fight the enemy in any way they chose, regardless of a commander's program. Paul Jones had stopped this threatened uprising by confining

Simpson below. On reaching port he had transferred him to the *Admiral*, a ship where the French put men of his type.

After Simpson had been imprisoned, an American agent named Hezekiah Ford, who disliked the Scotch captain, got up a petition condemning Paul Jones and praising the conduct of Simpson in the sea fight. By smooth arguments to the effect that they would never get their prize money unless Lieutenant Simpson were made captain in place of Paul Jones, Ford induced seventy-eight of the *Ranger's* crew to sign this petition. The result was, that the rascally lieutenant was freed at his court-martial, and sailed away a little later for America, as master of the refitted *Ranger*.

When Paul Jones heard of the doings of Hezekiah Ford, he was terribly incensed. Tucking three pistols in his belt, he betook himself to the inn where Ford stopped. Without pausing long enough to draw even one of his pistols, he knocked Ford down with a lightning-like blow of his fist, seized the coachman's whip and thrashed the scoundrel until he cried for mercy. Big, long-limbed, weighing half as much again as Paul Jones, he offered no resistance—just curled up and blubbered like the coward he was, while the onlookers cheered the Scotchman with keen delight. Six months later, following other discoveries of his duplicity, Ford was denounced as a spy and traitor by the governor of Virginia, and Congress dishonorably dismissed him from the service after he had fled to London with valuable papers.

Before the *Ranger* sailed under the captaincy of Mr. Simpson, Paul Jones had met the expenses of her crew with the utmost difficulty. The credit obtained from his French friends did not meet all the heavy obligations, and after a while, in order to keep his men from starving, he was forced to sell the *Drake* at auction to a French ship-broker. This act was strictly against the rules and regulations of his country, but in the dire need of his crew and prisoners he felt that extreme measures must be adopted to raise the funds which he could get in no other manner. With this money he managed to pay off all indebtedness, and so it was with a clear conscience, if a bitter heart, that he saw the sly Simpson finally make off with his own ship, and many of his crew, leaving him alone in a foreign land.

War had now broken out between England and France, and Paul Jones was detained in Europe at the request of the French Minister of Marine. This official, De Sartine, wished an important command to be assigned to the famous conqueror of the *Drake*. The difficulties in the way, however, were great. The American commissioners had few resources, in addition to which one of them—Lee—was hostile to the Scotchman; and the French had more native officers clamoring for the better ships than they had such vessels.

Thus, about all that could be offered was the command of small warships or privateers, offers which the proud Jones promptly rejected. To M. Chaumont he wrote, in this connection, a letter containing the following extracts: "I wish to have no connection with any ship that does not sail fast, for I intend to go *in harm's way*. Therefore buy a frigate with sails fast, and that is sufficiently large to carry twenty-six or twenty-eight guns on her deck. I would rather be shot ashore than go to sea in the armed prizes I have described."

He continued his heckling correspondence with the greatest energy, alternately cajoling, proposing, complaining, begging to be sent on some important enterprise. He wrote innumerable letters to De Sartine, Franklin, De Chartres, De Chaumont, and many others, and finally to the king himself, who granted him an interview. More as a result of this conference with Louis XV than from other sources, he was finally rewarded by being put in command of a small squadron.

At first he was highly delighted with the appointment, but as time wore on and he saw what a poor assortment of ships and crews he had, he was vastly disappointed. But having accepted the command, with true heroic purpose he made up his mind to carry it through to the best of his ability.

The expense of fitting out the expedition was the king's, while the flag and the commissions of the officers were American. The object of the French government was to get Paul Jones to operate against the coasts and shipping of England under the American flag, as the courtesy of warfare forbade France, as an ally, to ravage the coasts of Great Britain before the enemy herself had struck a blow at French interests.

As stated, Paul Jones had a motley array of ships—those which were left over after the French officers had had their pick. The flag-ship, the *Bon Homme Richard*, was a worn-out old East Indiaman, which he refitted and armed with six 18-pounders, twenty-eight 12-pounders, and eight 9-pounders—a battery of forty-two guns. The crew consisted of 375 men of many nationalities, among which were not more than one hundred and fifty Americans, including Wannashego, who had faithfully stuck to his leader during all his trials in Brest. The *Alliance*, the only American ship, was a good frigate rating as a large thirty-two or medium thirty-six. She was commanded by a jealous-minded, half-mad Frenchman named Landais, who was in the American service. The *Pallas*, thirty-two guns; the *Vengeance*, twelve guns; and the little *Cerf*, of eight guns, were all officered and manned by Frenchmen.

Bad as were conditions of ship and crew, however, there was one other feature of the organization which proved a greater handicap to the Scotch commodore. This was the famous *concordat*, an agreement between the various commanders of the ships which Paul Jones was compelled to sign before his commission would be approved by the French minister of the navy. While its terms related largely to the distribution of prize money, it also contained clauses which weakened his authority, and gave his captains a chance to wink at it if they chose.

The little squadron, accompanied by two French privateers, sailed finally from L'Orient on August 14, 1779, on what was planned to be a fifty-days' cruise. Thanks to the Duchesse De Chartres's gift of ten thousand louis d'or, Paul Jones had been able to fit out his flag-ship in a much better condition than the king's fund would have permitted.

On the 18th the privateer *Monsieur,* which was not bound by the *concordat,* took a prize which the captain of that vessel proceeded to relieve of all valuables and then ordered into port. The commodore opposed this, and sent the prize to L'Orient. This so angered the *Monsieur's* captain that he parted company with the squadron.

But the episode was only the beginning of Paul Jones's troubles with insubordination of officers. While attempting to capture a brigantine, some of his English sailors deserted in two of his small boats. These could not be overhauled, and Landais insolently upbraided the commodore for their loss, declaring that thereafter he would act entirely upon his own responsibility (which indeed he had been doing right along!). The *Cerf* and the other privateer then pretended to go off to look for the escaped former English prisoners, and they too failed to appear again.

Paul Jones was now left with only the *Bon Homme Richard,* the *Pallas,* the *Vengeance,* and the *Alliance.* It would have been better, as later events showed, if the latter ship had decamped with the *Cerf* and the privateers; for Captain Landais impudently ignored all of Paul Jones's signals. He even had the audacity to leave the squadron for several days at a time, as the cruise continued, returning when the whim seized him. When other prizes were taken he was bold enough to send two of these into Bergen, Norway, where they were sold to the English, a procedure entirely against the wishes of the commodore, and one which was a source of trouble between Denmark and the United States for many years after the war.

Paul Jones was also compelled to humor the other French captains. Several times he changed his course or modified his operations in compliance with their demands. Had he enjoyed an absolute command he would have carried out his pet scheme of laying Leith and Edinburgh under contribution, but he was so afraid that such a venture would miscarry, owing to the uncertain behavior of his men, that he gave it up.

With his old flag-ship, his ragged squadron, and his unruly officers, Paul Jones then cruised along the Yorkshire coast, and succeeded in capturing a number of vessels. Finally, as he was preparing to end his disappointing voyage at The Texel, Holland, in accordance with Dr. Franklin's orders, chance threw in his way the opportunity for making the cruise a brilliant success.

And, Jones-like, this opportunity he seized eagerly. He saw in a flash that it was his one moment for restoring his waning power to its former pinnacle.

XIII

FIGHTING FRIEND AND FOE

It was on the 23d of September, when the squadron was chasing a small ship off Flamborough Head, that a number of distant sails were seen rounding the point. A long, steady look through his glass convinced Commodore Jones that he could not be mistaken: that this was the Baltic fleet of merchantmen which he had heard were in that vicinity, and which he had hoped he might meet before he reached The Texel.

Without delay Paul Jones hoisted the signal for a general chase. Captain Landais, however, ignored the signal, and sailed on by himself. So angry was Paul Jones at this cool display of indifference—or cowardice, if that it were,—that he stamped his foot on the deck, and shouted his feelings through his speaking-trumpet, but it availed nothing; the insolent Landais kept right on going.

When the merchant ships saw Paul Jones's squadron bearing down upon them, they ran in under the lee of the shore, and, protected by two British frigates which immediately got in between them and their foe, made off down the coast at their best speed. These English frigates were the *Serapis*, a brand-new ship of forty-four guns, and the *Countess of Scarborough*, twenty guns.

**FIGHT BETWEEN THE SERAPIS AND THE BON HOMME
RICHARD**
From a rare print

The afternoon sun was well down in the heavens by this time. In the far distance, her sails glinting white and rosy in the path of the sun, and constantly growing smaller, was the fleeing *Alliance*. And not far behind her, in pursuit, sped the little *Vengeance*, whose captain Paul Jones had told to try to persuade the half-mad Landais to return to his duty.

This turn of affairs left two ships facing each other on each side. Commodore Jones ordered Captain Cottineau, of the *Pallas*, to look after the *Countess of Scarborough*, while he himself took care of the *Serapis*. He never lost his head; with that "cool, determined bravery," of which Benjamin Franklin spoke, and with "that presence of mind which never deserted him," recorded by Fanning, he made up his mind to make the best of a seemingly hopeless situation, and engage an enemy ship which he knew to be the superior of his own in almost every respect.

He now crowded on all possible sail, until the *Bon Homme Richard* had come within pistol shot of the *Serapis*. It was then seven o'clock and the moon was just rising in a clear blue sky. Off some distance, the *Countess* had begun to run away, and the little *Pallas* was making after her fiercely. Paul Jones was thus left practically alone to meet his big antagonist of the bristling guns and well-trained, perfectly-disciplined crew.

As the *Bon Homme Richard* approached him, Captain Pearson, of the *Serapis*, hailed; but there was no reply. "I don't like this fellow's looks, for all he is apparently less powerful than ourselves," observed the British commander to his first officer. Uneasily he used his night-glass again. "I wonder if it can be the blood-thirsty pirate, Paul Jones," he added a moment later. Then he ordered his sailing-master to hail again.

"This is His Majesty's ship *Serapis*, forty-four guns. What ship is that?"

Still no answer.

Once more the hail came over the water, sharper, more peremptorily. "This is His Maj——"

By this time Paul Jones had the *Bon Homme Richard* where he wanted her; he gave a low signal to Richard Dale, who commanded the *Richard's* gun-deck, and Lieutenant Dale cried, "Blow your matches, boys!" At his words the gunners touched a tiny flame to the touch-hole of each big gun on the port side, and a heavy broadside was poured into the enemy ship.

But the British captain was not far behind. Before the echoes had died out his own guns spat fire with a roar, and great clouds of smoke drifted up and began to envelope the combatants. Following this the discharges came fast and furious, both the American and British crews working their guns with the utmost vigor.

From the beginning the fight seemed to go against the *Bon Homme Richard*. There was hardly any stage of the three and a half hours' desperate combat at which Paul Jones would not have been excused in lowering his flag—had he not been the prodigious fighter he was. Hardly had the battle well begun when two of the rust-pitted old 18-pounders exploded, killing the men working them and rendering the whole battery useless for the rest of the action.

Perceiving this, and anxious to take advantage of the loss of defense on the lower gun-deck resulting, Captain Pearson attempted again to pass the bow of the *Richard* and rake her. On the other hand, Commodore Jones's whole effort was to close with the enemy and board him, for he knew now that it was only a question of time, if he did not succeed, before his old shell of a vessel would be sunk.

After the broadsiding had continued with unremitting fury for almost an hour, Captain Pearson made another effort to get across the *Richard's* bow. But he miscalculated, and the two vessels were brought so close together that the *Richard* ran into her enemy's weather quarter. Paul Jones was quick to make his first attempt to board, but the ships swung apart before the operation could be completed, and those who had reached the *Serapis's* rail had to leap back to save themselves from capture.

The *Bon Homme Richard* was now in a sad condition. Little of her starboard battery was left, and of the 140 odd officers and men stationed at the main gun-deck battery at the beginning, over eighty had been killed or wounded. Numerous holes low in the hull, made by the big balls of the *Serapis's* 18-pound guns, were letting in water at an alarming rate. Time and time again did the ship's carpenter and his mate stop these up, only to have new holes splinter through with a sickening sound.

It is no wonder that Captain Pearson, knowing his enemy was in great distress, thought that, when the crew of the other ship had failed to board him, Commodore Jones would be ready to surrender.

"Has your ship struck?" he called through his trumpet.

And then Paul Jones made his famous reply:

"I have not yet begun to fight!"

After the ships had swung apart they continued to fire broadsides into each other. With the starboard battery of the *Richard* practically out of commission, however, it is easy to see that she worked at a great disadvantage in this sort of dueling. Had not a lucky wind favored her at this stage, it is likely she could not have floated much longer. This enabled her to blanket her enemy, which compelled the *Serapis* to lose all headway.

By more adroit handling of his vessel, waterlogged though she was, Paul Jones once more brought the ships alongside, bow to bow and stern to stern.

"Now, my fine fellows, lash us together!" cried the commodore; and with his own hands he helped his men to do the job, while the muskets of the British sailors rattled a storm of lead among them.

At this critical time, when Paul Jones was bending every nerve to grapple with the *Serapis*, the renegade *Alliance* suddenly made her appearance. The hearts of the gallant commander and his brave lads beat gladly at this sight. "Now," thought they, "Landais has come back to help us!"

Judge of their dismay when, as soon as he could get within range, the mad French captain turned his broadsides not into the British frigate but into the already sorely-afflicted *Bon Homme Richard*! She staggered under the fresh onslaught, the vicious bite of him who should have given aid. The American sailors cursed the treacherous Landais, and shook their fists at him. If they could have caught him they would have rended him limb from limb, so violent was their rage. In the midst of the maledictions, the culprit turned about and made away again, with the strange fickleness of purpose that had all along characterised his movements.

As soon as the *Serapis* and the *Richard* were well lashed together, Paul Jones drew practically all his crew from below to the upper deck and the tops, leaving only a small force to man the three small pieces on the quarter-deck. From this upper position they now commenced sweeping the decks of the enemy with their muskets. The crew of the *Serapis*, on the other hand, were forced to take refuge on their lower decks, from which point they continued to fire their great guns into the already riddled hull and lower decks of the *Richard*.

Several times Captain Pearson made desperate attempts to cut the lashings loose, but at each of these efforts the fire of the American ship's muskets was so accurate and withering that British seamen fell one upon another. Not a single British Jack reached the coveted goal, if we may except one bold fellow who was just opening his heavy Sheffield knife to sever the key-rope when an unerring bullet from the watchful Wannashego cut short his life. In another instance, the young Indian saw a British sailor drawing a bead on Paul Jones, who stood all unconscious of his peril. There was a report—but it was the report of Wannashego's reliable gun instead, and the British marine tumbled from the rigging where he was concealed.

Soon all the officers of the French marines had been killed or wounded, and Paul Jones was forced to take charge of them. His voice cheered them on in their own tongue; he exhorted them to take good aim, and when he saw a fellow firing ineffectively, he would often take his musket from his hand and show him, by coolly bringing down one of the foe, how he should manipulate it. In fact, toward the last the commodore stood on the quarter-deck rail by the main topmast backstay, and as he gave orders and encouragement, received loaded muskets from his marines, and fired them with deadly precision. His indomitable spirit penetrated every quaking soul, infusing it with new hope and new courage. As one French sailor said afterward: "Everyone who saw his example or heard his voice became as much a hero as Paul Jones himself."

By this time both vessels were on fire in several places. Half the men on both ships had been killed or disabled. The leaks in the *Richard's* hold had multiplied, she was much deeper in the sea; while the mainmast of the *Serapis* hung in splinters and threatened to go by the board at any moment.

Now, to the surprise of everybody, the cowardly Landais, with the *Alliance*, once more put in an appearance. This time he fired several broadsides into both combatants, seeming to take as much delight in hitting one as the other. As before, the man who surely could not have been sane, put his helm over and sailed away—very luckily for the last time.

While he was making off, a gunner on the *Richard*, thinking the ship was sinking, called loudly for quarter. No sooner were the words out of his mouth than Paul Jones sprang forward and felled him with the butt end of his pistol.

"Do you want quarter?" called Captain Pearson.

"No," roared Paul Jones; "you are the one to ask that!" And he purposely sent a pistol shot whistling close to the British captain's ears.

As if to make matters worse at this trying moment, the master-at-arms on the *Richard*, also thinking the ship sinking, opened the hatches and released nearly two hundred British prisoners, taken from prizes, who began to swarm on deck in the greatest confusion!

It was a moment to try the resourcefulness of the quickest intellect. Paul Jones hesitated just a moment, then he thundered at the prisoners to man the pumps or he would fill them full of lead. They obeyed like dumb-driven sheep. As the water in the hold of the sinking ship began to pour over her bulwarks into the sea again, the men on the *Richard* resumed the battle with new vigor.

Paul Jones had given orders to drop hand-grenades from the rigging down into the hold of the *Serapis*, through her main hatchway, which was open. By this same means the enemy had been set afire at various times before. Now, at an opportune moment, a hand-grenade fell among a pile of cartridges strung out on the deck of the *Serapis*. A terrific explosion occurred, killing many of her men.

It was an opportunity too good to let go. With a shout, the dashing John Mayrant, cleared the bulwarks of the enemy ship at the head of a yelling throng of Americans and French, and the next moment a terrific hand-to-hand struggle with cutlass and pistol was being waged.

BOARDING THE SERAPIS
From a rare print

Seeing his men falling back, Captain Pearson knew that he was a defeated man, and struck his colors to save those of his crew still alive.

The capture of the British frigate came none too soon, for the old shot-torn *Bon Homme Richard* was settling fast. By the combined efforts of crew and prisoners, the fire in both ships was extinguished. Then all bent their efforts to removing the wounded and prisoners from the *Richard* to the *Serapis*, together with ammunition and other valuables.

All the rest of that night the heroic old craft kept afloat, with the Stars-and-Stripes—the same flag the Colonial maids of Portsmouth had given Paul Jones upon his departure in the *Ranger*—flying proudly at her peak. Then, as if waiting for daylight to illuminate her last action before man, she slowly sank just as the sun came up across the waters in the east. The very last vestige anybody saw of her was her flag, still flying—unstruck!

When, two years later, Paul Jones returned to America, he met Miss Mary Langdon, who had been one of the girls to make this ensign. "I wished above all things to bring this flag to America," said he; "but, Miss Mary, I could not bear to strip the old ship in her last agony, nor could I deny to my dead on her decks, who had given their lives to keep it flying, the glory of taking it with them."

"You have done exactly right, commodore," exclaimed she. "That flag is just where we all wish it to be—flying at the bottom of the sea over the only ship that ever went down in victory!"

XIV

DIPLOMACY AND SOCIETY

The desperate battle fought in the bright moonlight was witnessed by many persons in Scarborough and on the Flamborough Head. These English people immediately spread the alarming tidings throughout the enemy country by lighting immense signal fires on the cliffs. Although it was not definitely known what ship had taken the formidable *Serapis*, nearly everybody rightly guessed that it had been captained by the "terrible Paul Jones." The British along the sea coast all the way from Cape Clear to Hull were in a great fright, and for days to come looked for the appearance of the "blood-thirsty buccaneer" in their particular locality.

With his two new prizes—for the *Pallas* had succeeded in capturing the *Countess of Scarborough* after a short engagement—the commodore now set off for The Texel, where he arrived October 3. He was none too soon in getting into port, either. Very shortly after his arrival an English squadron, consisting of sixty-four ships-of-the-line and three heavy frigates, which had been looking for him, hove into view.

The scape-goat Landais, with the *Alliance*, was already in The Texel when the American-French squadron arrived. Paul Jones at once took steps for the care of the wounded and prisoners, and then sent special messengers to Dr. Franklin with news of the great victory and a report of Landais's scandalous behavior, demanding that he be court-martialed.

An important problem now to be solved was how to induce the Dutch authorities to allow Paul Jones and his battered ships to remain long enough in a neutral port to make necessary repairs to carry them to France. Indeed, Sir Joseph Yorke, British minister in Holland, lost no time in demanding that the Dutch government turn over to England "the pirate and criminal, Paul Jones, and every ship under his command." An enormous amount of correspondence then passed between the diplomats of the three countries concerned; conferences were held; even Paul Jones himself took a most active hand in presenting his arguments in favor of the step he had taken. The people of Holland were secretly in sympathy with the revolting colonies; but the wealthy Dutch ship-owners were gaining a rich harvest from the commerce with England at this time, and they made their weighty power felt in settling the question. These men thought the ships should be held by Holland until after the war. However, the other contingent argued them down, and the States-General at last sent England the verdict of his country, which was to the effect that Holland would *not* deliver over the vessels to England, but would insist that they depart from Holland waters at the first favorable weather.

In the meantime, kind-hearted Dutch maids thronged the decks of the *Serapis*, *Alliance*, *Pallas* and *Scarborough*. They brought with them gifts of food and clothing for the strong and healthy, as well as an abundance of delicacies for the sick and wounded. More than one rosy-cheeked, fair-haired girl acted as nurse, and it is no wonder that under such jolly, tender care the ailing ones made rapid improvement.

As he watched his ships nearing the finish of their repairs, Paul Jones's heart became more anxious, and often he looked seaward where the British ships were grimly patrolling to prevent his escape when the Dutch authorities should order him out at the first favorable wind. He hoped intensely that this sort of wind would not come before he had everything aboard in readiness and his plans for evading the enemy well formed.

On the 13th of December the French minister of marine, De Sartine, demanded that he should fly the French flag, which naturally commanded greater respect from Holland than the American ensign. In vain he expostulated to this gentleman and to Dr. Franklin, his friend in Paris; the latter stated he thought it the best thing to do. Therefore, Paul Jones made the change, but with great reluctance. It grieved him deeply to see the flag of another country, other than that under which the *Serapis* had had to bow down to, fluttering at her masthead.

Close upon the heels of this disappointment came another to tear the heartstrings of the irritated Scotchman. This was an order for him to relinquish supervision of all his ships except the *Alliance*, which he was to command as an ordinary captain. The *Serapis* he must turn over to Captain Cottineau, who, it was said, would look after the fortunes of this vessel, as well as the *Pallas* and the *Vengeance* and the *Scarborough*, in the future. Commodore Jones sent vehement protestations at this humiliating change to the French government and the American commissioners, but in vain; no other arrangement could well be made, wrote Dr. Franklin. So our hero bowed in submission, although when he went aboard the *Alliance* as her captain he defiantly pulled down the French flag at her peak and ran up the Stars-and-Stripes.

The incessant jangling and wrangling with the diplomats of three countries in addition to his own, had made Paul Jones very sore at heart. Therefore, he was very glad when, on Christmas Day, 1779, the weather underwent a change which promised him a chance to get away from The Texel. That morning he awoke to find such a gale blowing that most of the patrolling English frigates were driven off the coast. All that day and the next it howled so furiously that he dared not venture to steal out himself; but early on the morning of the 27th he made a dash in the *Alliance*, boldly shaping his course for the Straits of Dover.

As daring as ever, he sailed down the English Channel, passing close to the Channel Fleet of the enemy. They gave chase, but he outmaneuvred them, and finally put in at Corunna, Spain, for repairs. On February 10, 1780, he sailed into L'Orient.

The following year was passed mainly in France, where Paul Jones applied himself energetically to trying to collect prize money for his men and himself, and trying to secure an important command. He wrote rather more than his usual large number of letters,—to Franklin, the Duchesse De Chartres, Robert Morris, Arthur Lee, Dr. Bancroft, and many others,—in an endeavor to carry out some of his pet plans for the betterment of war operations. In spite of his hard efforts to collect this prize money, there were many annoying delays caused by technicalities, and his crew as a whole grew impatient and rebellious. This feeling was increased when the traitor, Landais, suddenly appeared among them, and abetted by Arthur Lee, stirred up the men with many lies.

Wannashego carried this state of affairs to Paul Jones as soon as he became convinced of the peril of the situation, but even while he was in quest of his friend, Landais and Lee went aboard and took possession of the ship. When, on his arrival, Paul Jones found what had transpired he was so angry that he could hardly contain himself. He came very near to shooting both the conspirators; but as usual when in a temper he calmed down with surprising quickness, and departed. The next day the *Alliance*, under the command of Landais, sailed for America, with Lee aboard. Paul Jones made no effort to prevent it. "Let them go," he said to Wannashego; "I am well rid of such a pair of precious scoundrels. As for the ship, she is not worth fighting over."

So Landais sailed away with the *Alliance*, but to his own ruin—something the astute Scotchman had foreseen. On the voyage Landais's eccentricity caused his friend Lee to put him under arrest, and on arrival in America a court of inquiry found him unfit for command, and he never burdened the service again.

Paul Jones had arrived in Paris this time in a blaze of fame. He was lionized by society, congratulated by royalty, was the idol of women high and low. He was bidden by the Duc and Duchesse De Chartres to be their guest at the Palais Royal, and occupied one of the splendid apartments of that historic dwelling during his stay in Paris. As soon as the Duchesse had received the commodore's letter acquainting her with his victory over the *Serapis*—in these words: "The enemy surrendered at thirty-five minutes past

10:00 p. m. by your watch, which I consult only to fix the moment of victory"—she prepared to give a great ball in his honor.

And now that Paul Jones was present in person, the charming Duchesse could not seem to do enough to attest her regard for him. She gave a wonderful banquet, with him as the chief guest. As the evening waned he asked her if she remembered his promise to lay an English frigate at her dainty feet. On hearing her assent, he turned to an attendant, who had been holding the sword surrendered by Captain Pearson, and taking this he dropped gracefully on one knee and presented it to the beautiful Duchesse with these words: "While I am unable to lay so large a thing as a frigate at the feet of your Royal Highness, I nevertheless am able to surrender to the loveliest of women the sword surrendered by one of the bravest of men on such a frigate."

Of course the petite Aimée De Telusson was present at this meeting, and to her, as usual, Paul Jones gallantly paid the most marked attention. His gayety was contagious. His wit was the wonder of all those assembled. With one and all he was a favorite, this son of a poor Scotch gardener.

XV

AND THE LAST

For some time Benjamin Franklin, knowing the need of supplies for Washington's army, had been soliciting Paul Jones to take command of the *Ariel* and transport such goods from France to America. But the Scotch commodore, dissatisfied with the humbleness of a command on such a small sloop, had held off stubbornly, hoping that in the meantime a ship of greater caliber and importance would be presented to him. Honors bestowed upon him by the King of France, wherein he had been presented with the Royal Order of Military Merit and a beautiful gold sword, seemed to have increased his native unbounded ambitions and to have almost spoiled him for anything but the most exalted of offices.

But on October 8, 1780, he finally sailed away in the *Ariel*, having a goodly number of his old crew with him, including his valiant young Indian friend Wannashego, who was now eager to see his home country and people, from whom he had been away just one month short of three years. The young Narragansett's muscles were like steel bands now, and not a member of the *Ariel's* crew could throw him. This had been amply attested in the wrestling bouts which took place on the eve of the ship's departure from L'Orient, when Commodore Jones had given an elaborate farewell party. On this occasion the little *Ariel* had been bewitchingly decorated from stern to bow, the finest people of France had been in attendance, and a wonderful mimic sham battle had been shown, a replica of that terrible fight between the *Bon Homme Richard* and the *Serapis*.

The little *Ariel* arrived in Philadelphia the 18th of February, 1781, and there her commander took affectionate leave of Wannashego. For five years the young Narragansett Indian had fought at Paul Jones's side, never once flinching, and therefore he seemed more like a younger brother than a friend. At this time the Scotchman himself was thirty-three years old.

Upon his arrival the commodore called on many of his friends, and then proposed having an investigation of the doings of his enemy, Arthur Lee. But his friends dissuaded him from this. With the whole country ringing his praises, as had been the case when he left France, it was easy for him to forgive his enemies. Congress passed resolutions in which they complimented him for his victories and service to the States, and a most appreciative letter was written him by the great George Washington himself.

It now seemed to Paul Jones a favorable time to improve his rank—an object he never lost sight of!—and on May 28 he sent a memorial to Congress reiterating his claims to stand above the captains who had been unjustly put ahead of him. He failed, probably on account of the political influence of the aforesaid captains; but he was rewarded with the command of the *America*, a fine new 74-gun ship-of-the-line then building at Portsmouth. He at once went to Portsmouth, and worked for weeks getting her ready for sea—only to have her turned over to the King of France!

With undaunted energy he now attempted to get hold of the *South Carolina*, formerly the *Indien*. But the plan failed, and he remained without a vessel. Unable to rest, although his health had for some time been failing, he was given consent to go off with the French fleet under Marquis De Vaudreuil, "in pursuit of military marine knowledge," as he termed his object. Then, in the summer of 1783, came an attack of fever. On his recovery, he was appointed by Congress as agent to collect all moneys due from the sale of prizes taken in European waters under his command. In this work he showed unusual business tact and ability.

When the war closed, he began a profitable business in illuminating oils, and continued his activities in securing prize money until all accounts had been settled. Then Paul Jones set off for Copenhagen to collect indemnity from the Danish government for the prizes the mad Landais had delivered to Bergen, and which that country had turned over to England before the declaration of hostilities between the two. He arrived in January, 1788, and was magnificently entertained by the court, being given a pension of 1500 crowns a year "for respect shown to the Danish flag" while he commanded in the European seas. The negotiations for indemnity were suspended and transferred, with his agreement, to Paris.

When Paul Jones was in Paris, the Russian ambassador to France made a proposition to him, through Mr. Jefferson, to take a position in the Russian navy. Russia was then at war with Turkey, and the clever Simolin so impressed the Scotch captain with the great deeds he might do for the benefit of the Russian empire and the distress of the Turks, that he at once began to maneuver for the highest command possible. He demurred at the rank of captain-commandant, a rank equal to that of brigadier-general in the present United States army—and maintained that nothing less than that of rear-admiral was fitting. This was allowed.

Our hero left Copenhagen on his ill-fated Russian mission, April 11, and made a flying and perilous trip to St. Petersburg. The Baltic was filled with ice blocks, but at the muzzle of his pistols the intrepid Scotchman forced two frightened and unwilling boatmen to row him across the turbulent stream. On April 23 he was presented to the Empress, and she conferred upon him the coveted rank of rear-admiral, to the profound disgust of many of the English officers in the service of Russia, who looked upon the newcomer as a red-handed and infamous pirate.

With many a jealous eye on him, Paul Jones departed from St. Petersburg on May 7, to take command of the Russian squadron in the Black Sea. But even while he was leaving envy and hate behind him, he was going forward into feeling even more bitter. His fortune put him in co-command with an arrogant adventurer, the Prince of Nassau, who at once became extremely jealous of the American. Nassau advised him to allow Prince Potemkin, in charge of the fleet, to take the credit for any success which might result from an engagement, and to hold his tongue—two things which Paul Jones's nature would not allow him to do.

It is not advisable to enter into the details of this campaign, but enough may be given to explain some of the difficulties the man from across the sea encountered. Following some unimportant engagements, Captain Pacha, whose fleet lay before Oczakow, protecting that Turk-infested town from the Russian ships, attempted to attack the Russian fleet. But one of his ships ran aground, and the others anchored in much confusion. Paul Jones then made such a fierce attack that the Turkish ships cut anchor and fled, with him in pursuit. He signaled Nassau to join him, but the latter paid no attention, and continued to fire inhumanely into two others of the enemy which were aground and ablaze. Paul Jones then continued on after the fleeing Turkish ships, many of which he captured or ran aground. Later on, the cowardly Nassau came up and proceeded to rake the helpless enemy fore and aft, killing most of their crews while they pleaded for quarter.

Paul Jones was so disgusted and incensed at this conduct that he publicly upbraided Prince Nassau, gaining his further ill-will, and bringing down upon his head a rebuke from the crafty Prince Potemkin. To add to his anger, when the Empress made her awards of bravery for this battle, Nassau received the warmest praise and a valuable estate, while Paul received only the mediocre award of the Order of St. Anne.

A little later the despotic Potemkin had made up his mind that he could not get along with the independent and fiery American seaman, and secured an order which sent him into the northern seas. This was practically a dismissal for Paul Jones, who returned to St. Petersburg in virtual disgrace. By this time, too, Empress Catherine had had her ears so filled with the lies of his enemies, who seemed to take delight in besmirching his character and causing him every annoyance possible, even to the extent of intercepting his mail, that she was sincerely anxious to get rid of the man whom she had only a little while before admired so greatly. She did not dare to do this openly, however, owing to his powerful influence in France, which she feared; so promised him an important command in the Baltic seas, a command which she secretly made up her mind should never come his way.

Patiently Paul Jones waited in his humble lodgings in St. Petersburg for this commission. Days rolled by. Weeks rolled by. Months began to multiply. While he waited, he was falsely accused, in March, 1789, of an atrocious crime, and forbidden to approach the palace of the Empress. But for the French ambassador, M. De Ségur, who had a strong influence with the Empress, and who proved that Paul Jones was the victim of a plot, it is hard to tell how he would have come out of this difficulty. As it was, Catherine once more received him graciously, with profuse apologies.

But Paul Jones's health, largely owing to the indignities heaped upon him in Russia, was now fast failing; he asked for two years' leave of absence, and it was granted. His services to that country were considerable, yet they have never to this day been recognized. As an instance of the ridiculous reports circulated about him, we will state that he was said to have murdered his nephew—a person who had never existed! Can we wonder that the sensitive soul of this brave man was shattered after his harrowing experiences? Can we wonder that his iron-clad constitution, which should have held life in him not less than four-score years, began to go to pieces when he was still a young man?

On August 18, 1789, Paul Jones left St. Petersburg, never to return, and never again to fight a battle for any nation. He was only forty-two years old, but though still brave in spirit, so undermined in physical strength that he remained in Paris and became a spectator rather than an actor in the great French Revolution, then taking place.

Acquainted with men of all nationalities and in the highest and most influential positions, Paul Jones, now that he could do little else, settled down to entertaining his friends and being entertained himself. Always he seemed happiest when with the charming Aimée De Telusson, who to the very end of his last hours remained ever with him, a faithful and devoted nurse. Had he continued to live in health and strength there is little doubt but that he would have taken this beautiful, unselfish, and loving girl, the daughter of a king, to be his wife, for of all his many warm women friends, with her he was ever the most tender and considerate.

A stranger to illness, a conqueror of troubles which had seemed far more formidable to him, Paul Jones never doubted his recovery. Even when the doctors shook their heads and said his left lung was entirely gone and the other affected, he smiled and did not give up. His wonderful Scotch constitution held out amazingly. A number of times it looked as if he would win his battle with Death, for he would rise from his bed and seem his old energetic self again.

But gradually his strength was sapped. On the afternoon of the 18th of July, 1792, when forty-five years old, he consigned himself to the inevitable, and, assisted by Gouverneur Morris, drew up his will. A few hours afterward, while he lay in bed, his great spirit quietly departed.

PAUL JONES'S LAST BURIAL
Midshipman escorting the casket to its final resting place, in Annapolis, April 24th, 1906

In 1905, the American Embassy in Paris exhumed the body of America's glorious hero, after it had lain hidden for one hundred and thirteen years in the abandoned Cemetery of St. Louis. Under escort of one of our finest naval squadrons the body was brought to the United States and buried with much ceremony in Arlington, the National Cemetery at Washington.